Basic Statistics

— FOR —

Educational Research

Basic Statistics

—— FOR ——
Educational Research

Second Edition

John A. Kaufhold, Ed.D.

and

Sumita S. Kaufhold, Ed.D.

iUniverse LLC
Bloomington

Basic Statistics for Educational Research
Second Edition

iUniverse books may be ordered through booksellers or by contacting:

iUniverse LLC
1663 Liberty Drive
Bloomington, IN 47403
www.iuniverse.com
1-800-Authors (1-800-288-4677)

ISBN: 978-1-4759-9794-1 (sc)
ISBN: 978-1-4759-9795-8 (ebk)

Printed in the United States of America

iUniverse rev. date: 07/15/2013

Contents

Chapter One

<u>Introduction To Research</u>

The first step in becoming an intelligent consumer of research is to develop a "Healthy Skepticism". This is a polite way of saying "Don't believe everything you read or hear." Learn to ask important questions such as "Who" "Why" "How" "Where" and "When". For example, everyone has heard the old television commercial "Four out of five dentists prefer Colgate toothpaste." A simple statement such as this requires several questions by the wise consumer. Some of these questions might be as follows:

1- <u>How large was the sample selected?</u> Was it just 5 dentists, 50 or 100? This is important because the larger the sample is, the greater the chances are that the results are valid (true). Conversely, smaller samples tend to produce more errors or more bias.

2- <u>Were the subjects who were surveyed voluntary or paid participants?</u> This gets to the question—"why?" Why did these people participate in the study? What did <u>they</u> get out of it? Certainly it is reasonable to assume that a paid participant might be more inclined to give a favorable response to a product if he were paid by the makers of that product. A volunteer participant on the other hand, might be more neutral in his response.

3- Who conducted the study? Was the study conducted by an independent, impartial agency or laboratory or was it conducted by the makers of Colgate toothpaste? The answer to this question would go a long way toward the believability of the advertisement.

4- Who were the dentists? Were they impartial? Maybe they were stockholders in the company. Maybe they were friends or relatives of the company officials. These factors alone could cause bias.

5- Where were the dentists from? Maybe they were from the same city in which Colgate toothpaste is manufactured. If so, could they be expected to give an unbiased answer?

Now that we've covered the people on the survey, next we have to look at the survey itself and answer several questions such as these:

1- What questions were on the survey? A smart researcher can "stack the deck" with questions designed to produce a favorable answer. Look at the following question-

> "Do you rate Coldgrate toothpaste as "superior", "outstanding", or just "above average"?

The results of this survey could then be reported in the following manner:

> WHEN SURVEYED 100 OUT OF 100 PEOPLE RATED COLGATE TOOTHPASTE BETWEEN 'ABOVE AVERAGE' AND 'SUPERIOR'. YOU WILL TOO!

2- Were there any other toothpastes mentioned on the survey? Was there a basis for comparison that was presented?

3- What was the language used in expressing the results? Was the language specific of was it intentionally vague? Look at the following statement of results.

"9 out of 10 patients prefer coldgrate toothpaste." A proper question to ask here might be—"Prefer it to what? A root canal? An all-night drilling?"

Before we get too ridiculous, we should bring this example to a close and return to the subject of research. Interestingly, the same type of questions applies when considering the results of educational research studies. The intelligent consumer should ask:

1- Who conducted the research and what qualifications do they have? In other words, is the researcher an authority on the subject? Does the person's background, educational level or experiences qualify them as an expert whose work we can believe? In answering this question, two pertinent examples come to mind.

Example 1—

Not too many years ago, there was a popular advertisement on TV for a reading program called, "Hooked on Phonics." The "experts" who endorsed the program were famous television personalities. A proper question one might ask would be "What are their qualifications for judging the educational effectiveness of this program?"

Sometimes, however, even qualifications that appear to be legitimate can also be suspect.

Example 2—

Former National Secretary of Education, William Bennett, has written several articles "exposing" the "deplorable" conditions of American Education. While one might consider Bennett an authority on education because of his lofty office; the truth of the matter is that he is not and has never been a teacher or an administrator in American public records. He was, in fact, a political appointee with no classroom experience.

2- <u>When was the research conducted?</u> Generally speaking, research conducted ten years past the present time is considered to be out of date for the simple reason that new knowledge or techniques may have been discovered in the intervening time. (the exception here is if the study was an historical study or if it involved a longitudinal approach over a period of years.)

3- <u>Where was the research conducted?</u> This can be a bit tricky and it might require a bit of knowledge about the research institution. Is the institution known as a conservative or a liberal place of study? Results of research might be tainted by the affiliation of the organization.

4- <u>What were the motivations for the study?</u> Was it part of a research grant? If so, what organization funded the grant? Did that organization have any vested interests in the results?

5- <u>How was the research conducted?</u> Did the researcher or researchers follow careful procedures to ensure the principles of validity and reliability?

One can see, therefore, that research results cannot just be taken at face value. If one or more of any of these questions are unanswered, the results of the research are open to question. Use of data from questionable sources can often lead to invalidation or nullification of results proposed to the reader. Objectively speaking, not all research that appears in print is good research. As in many other fields, imperfections exist—professors doing hurried research in an effort to gain promotion, graduate students striving to prove research questions to finish dissertations, grant workers anxious to conclude a project before the grant money is dissolved. While most researchers ARE legitimate, however, it behooves the wise consumer to be cautious.

Research Terminology

Before one can begin to understand research methodology, it is necessary to first learn some of the language of research. The following are common terms found in most research studies.

1- Subject—A subject is who or what is studied or examined in the research project. In most studies, the number of subjects is indicated by a small "n". Always look for n=. This tells the number of subjects. Generally speaking, the larger the number of subjects, the less chance of statistical error or bias.

2- Variable—A variable is anything in a study that changes and can be measured. A variable can also be anything that affects the subject. Examples of variables that change and can be measured are academic or physical achievement, classroom behavior, attitudes.

3- Dependent Variable—This is the variable that the researchers are trying to change. In most educational studies, the researcher is trying to increase learning or improve behavior; these, then are dependent variables.

4- Independent Variable—The independent variable affects the dependent variable and brings about a difference or a change. An example of an independent variable might be the introduction of technology to the classroom through the use of a computer in the hope that it may increase learning. Hopefully the introduction of this independent variable will positively affect the dependent variable (learning).

5- Extraneous Variable—This is an unplanned variable that affects the dependent variable and influences the results of the study EVEN THOUGH IT HAS NOTHING TO DO WITH THE STUDY. An example of an extraneous variable might be heat or cold. Because of an excessively hot classroom, students might be unable to concentrate while working on a computer thus, this unplanned variable might affect their learning and distort the results of the study.

Note: There are a HOST of extraneous variables that could distort the results of a study. Some of these are: the time of day, the time of year (before a holiday, after a holiday), a big event (prom, football game, etc.) the skill (or lack of skill) that a teacher has, teachers' personalities, ad infinatum. It is the researcher's job to eliminate or account for these variables as she compiles her results.

6- <u>Bias</u>—Bias is an unintentional systematic error that is introduced into the sampling that causes an invalid result. An example of bias might occur if two unequal groups of subjects are studied. One group might be more intelligent than another and, thus, the comparison might be flawed (this would be the case if the researcher wrongly assumed that the groups were equal).
Another type of bias is the unintended prejudice of the researcher. In this case, the researcher might have certain feelings or beliefs that may sway his or her judgment of the findings or results. Another instance might be where the researcher's prejudice may cause him or her to only look for one type of result or to examine only one side of the issue. Thus a person who strongly believes in the INCLUSION of special education children in the regular classroom may only examine the positive effects of this practice or else give undue emphasis to the positive results it produces.

7- <u>Experimental Group</u>—In experimental research involving two or more groups of subjects, the experimental group is the group that receives special treatment. For example in a research study that tests the use of computers (independent variable) to increase learning (dependent variable) the experimental group would get special "treatment" (the use of computer).

8- <u>Control Group</u>—In experimental research involving two or more groups of subjects, the control group receives NO special treatment. In the example previously mentioned, the control group would be taught in a conventional manner WITHOUT the use of computers. The results of the study would then be examined to see if the use of computers caused increased learning in the experimental group.

Note: To verify that the increased learning was actually the result of the independent variable (the computers); the subjects in the control group are switched to the experimental group and vice-versa. If the results are the same for the "new" experimental group then it can be shown that the independent variable (the computers) was, indeed the cause of the results. (assuming that any extraneous variables have been taken into consideration).

9- Population—The population is the defined group to which the researcher wants to apply the results. For example, a researcher might want to make a study of dropout prevention techniques for ninth grade students in a school district.

10- Sample Population—The sample population is the portion of the population studied. In the previous example it may not be feasible to study all of the ninth grade students in the school district—especially if the school district is very large. Instead, the researcher may only study a sample of the entire population.

11- Generalizability—This is the degree to which the results of a study with one sample can be applied to the defined population. For example, if a study was correctly and carefully done and if the demographics of the sample closely matched the demographics of the population, the results of the study of a sample of ninth grade students could be applied (generalized) to the entire ninth grade population.

Note: If these demographics DO NOT match closely, however, the results could be biased and would be considered to be invalid.

12- <u>Hypotheses</u>—In scientific research, the hypothesis is a statement that describes how the researcher expects the results to turn out. It is a statement of what the researcher is trying to prove. The purpose of the research, therefore, is to <u>prove</u> or <u>disprove</u> the hypothesis. An example of a hypothesis might be the following statement:

Hypothesis—the use of personal computers in a 5th grade classroom will produce a statistically significant increase in the achievement of learners.

13- <u>Statistical Significance</u>—Statistical significance is determined by the application of statistical procedures to see if THE SAME RESULTS would occur if the study was repeated using another sample for the same population. In other words, if the researcher repeated the study, what are the CHANCES that the results would be the same with a different group?

Note: In most research studies, statistical significance is reached at the .05 or .01 level. This means that the results of the study are 95% accurate (.05) or 99% accurate (.01) Another way to say this is that .05 is the same as 5/100 or five one-hundredths. Therefore there are only FIVE chances in 100 that the results are incorrect. For .01, there is only ONE chance in 100 that the results are not true. Most researchers will commonly accept this degree of accuracy in research results. Typically, results are reported in the study in this fashion.

Types and Methods of Research

Research consists of various types and various methods. The types of research are general categories while the methods of research are specific ways of conduction a research study.

Basic/Theoretical Research

These terms are actually synonymous but for the purpose of clarity, only the term theoretical research will be used. Theoretical research is usually conducted by scholars or professional researchers whose only role is research. Often, they do little or no teaching. Their research is conducted either in a laboratory setting or in a similar controlled environment. The purpose of this research is solely to contribute to the development of new knowledge.

These researchers, therefore, are interested in expanding the scope of the knowledge base of a field of study. They are not concerned with the application phase. Many of the research findings attributed to these researchers or "research scientists" constitute the chapters of college textbooks or appear in government publications. B.F. Skinner, whose theories of behavioral psychology have been used in educational classrooms for fifty years, conducted his experimental research in laboratories of universities. His subjects were rats, pigeons and human beings. Skinner's role was to experiment and publish his findings in the areas of education and psychology.

Jean Piaget, on the other hand was a Swiss psychologist who was interested in child development theory. He developed his principles by working with children and young adults in a controlled school-type setting in Switzerland. Research scientists such as Lawrence Kohlberg and Jerome Bruner conducted experimental basic research at Harvard University.

Action, Applied, Empirical Research

Once again, these terms can be used synonymously. To eliminate confusion the term action research will be used. Unlike basic or theoretical research, action research is conducted by practitioners and is applied to a specific setting. Practitioners are considered to be anyone who is actively engaged in the process of education. Thus, the practitioner could be a college professor, a classroom teacher, or a school administrator. The scope of the research could be large or as small as a single classroom.

The purpose of this research is to improve the teaching and learning environment here and now. While the research results might appear in a textbook or an educational journal. The application is meant to be immediate. It is important to note that most educational researchers from university professors to graduate students work on ACTION RESEARCH projects.

Quantitative Research

Quantitative research is the collection and analysis of NUMERICAL data in order to explain or predict topics of interest. Quantitative research, therefore, deals with NUMBERS and STATISTICS in order to answer research questions or to prove or disprove hypotheses. Quantitative research can be used in BOTH theoretical research and action research. Here again, it is important to note that MOST researchers use quantitative research. Numerical data are relatively easy to collect and, due to their factual composition, are objective and fairly easy to understand. When reading research reports many public officials and educational decision-makers like to refer to factual data.

Qualitative Research

Qualitative research, on the other hand, is the collection, analysis and INTERPRETATION of comprehensive narrative and visual data in order to gain INSIGHTS into a topic of interest. Qualitative data, therefore, deals with NON-NUMERICAL data in order to answer research questions or to prove or disprove hypotheses. Like quantitative research, qualitative research can be used in BOTH theoretical studies and action studies.

Due to the difficulty and time-consuming task of collecting this type of data MOST researchers prefer not to use this approach exclusively. Generally speaking, qualitative data MAY lack the objectivity of numerical studies and the results can be difficult to prove conclusively. Because the results are normally in narrative form, they are more laborious to read than a study based on pure facts or statistics.

Mixed Methods Research

In order to compensate for the difficulties inherent in qualitative studies, many researchers prefer to use a combination of quantitative and qualitative research. That is to say, a researcher may collect factual data employing numbers and statistics and, once this is done, employ a qualitative approach to "dig deeper" into the subject. What is meant by this is that a researcher may uncover facts in order to prove or disprove a series of questions or hypotheses and then do a follow-up analysis using qualitative data. In this instance, the quantitative data describe "what" occurred in the project while the qualitative portion answers the question "why" the results occurred.

A brief example of this approach might be as follows: During any sort of public election, data might be collected to determine HOW groups of people voted. How did women vote? How did men vote? How did young people vote, middle aged people vote, senior citizens vote? All of this data would be compiled and categorized. Still, the question remains—WHY did they vote the way they did? To answer this question, the researcher would employ a qualitative approach. The researcher, with the use of trained assistants, would go out and interview a representative sample of those who voted. Through face-to-face contact (or possible a telephone interview) the researchers would ask in-depth probing questions in order to ascertain WHY the voters responded the way they did. This data would be presented in narrative form and results would be INTERPRETED and explained.

Methods of Research

While the quantitative, qualitative and mixed methods approaches indicate the general TYPES of research, the specific METHODS of research are quite varied. A brief description of these methods follows.

Descriptive Research

Broadly speaking, descriptive research entails presenting an objective, unbiased account of a subject or a situation. In other words, this type of research determines and reports the way things are with a group of subjects or with certain conditions.

Correlation Research

Correlation research studies the relationship between two or more variables. For example, is there a relationship between a student's score on the SAT examinations and his GPA (grade point average) in college? Test makers at the Educational Testing Service have shown that a statistical correlation exists between these two variables and, thus, the SAT is used as a PREDICTOR of a student's future success in college. In like manner, correlation research can also be used in the classroom to see if there is a relationship between students' scores on a pre-algebra readiness test and scores on end-of-grade tests. If these scores correlate, the researcher could say that the pre-algebra test used is a good PREDICTOR of future success in algebra.

Causal-Comparative (ex-post facto) Research

While correlational research explores the future and allows predictions, causal-comparative research examines the past and attempts to explain the cause of a condition or an event. In this case, events are studied after-the-fact (ex-post facto). For example, causal-comparative research might be used to study why one group of students dropped out of high school while another similar group attained a diploma. Since events here occurred in the past, no variables can be manipulated in the study.

Experimental Research

In experimental types of research, the researcher CAN manipulate the variables in order to ascertain the effects of one variable on another. Experimental research involves the use of two groups of subjects with dependent and independent variables. For example, a researcher might want to see if the use of a different method of teaching promotes increased learning in students.

The students would then be divided into two groups. One group would be the experimental group and the other group would be the control group. The experimental group would get the "treatment"—the new teaching method. The control group would get nothing. That is to say they would be taught in the regular way. If, at the conclusion of the study, it could be proved STATISTICALLY that the experimental group learned more than the control group, the researcher could say that the "treatment"—the new method resulted in greater learning.

Another way of saying this is that the independent variable (the new method) affected the dependent variable (learning) in a positive manner. Some restrictions apply, however, if the results are presented as being valid. First, random sampling has to be used in the study. That is, both groups must have similar characteristics and should be evenly matched

13

as much as possible. Secondly, when possible, the variable should be MANIPULATED from one group to another. This means that the students in the control group should be switched with those in the experimental group. If the same results are obtained with a different group of students, it could be shown that the independent variable was the cause.

Quasi-Experimental Research

Unfortunately, parents have the quaint notion that they send their children to school to be educated and not to act as participants in research. This means that before experimental research is conducted in a classroom, parental permission must be acquired. If some parents refuse permission, this may alter the random requirement of the sample (not all students have an equal chance to be in the sample). When this event occurs and the sample is "tainted" the research must be called quasi-experimental.

Historical Research

Historical research, quite simply is the study of events in history for the purpose of comparison to present day life, understanding the origins of practices and behaviors or explaining the cause-effect relationships of conditions. This research differs from causal-comparative research in the type of data studied. Historical sources of data might be written documents such as original letters, diaries, records, articles or newspaper accounts. By this study, the researcher would piece together information form the past in order to answer the proposed research questions.

Case Study (Single-Subject) Research

Case study research involves the intensive study of an individual or group of individuals in a naturalistic setting that permits the researcher to describe the results in a qualitative way. Close observation is involved over an elongated period of time. Extreme care must be taken in this type of research to avoid any interruptions in the natural behavior of the subjects.

Summary

In this chapter, rudimentary tenets of research were presented. Included were the basic terminologies of research principles as well as a brief description of the methods and types of research. These principles will be presented in greater detail in subsequent chapters. The following chapter presents the beginning steps in conduction of a research study.

Chapter 2

Deciding on a Topic

Deciding on a proper research topic is perhaps the most difficult task for one who is about to embark on the writing of a thesis or a complete dissertation. Since the research and the subsequent chore of writing may require a lengthy period of time, the correct selection of the topic is crucial.

Before one chooses a topic to research, It is well to examine several important criteria. These criteria are:

a- interest
b- time
c- available supporting research
d- value to the profession
e- value to the researcher

Each of these will be answered in turn. Interest—Presumably, the researcher will spend a good deal of time working on his or her research project. Thorough research is not done over just a month or two. Since the research process is, by nature, tedious, it is advisable that the topic chosen should be one of high interest to the researchers. Research that is conducted in the vein of expediency often leads to boredom, frustrations and ultimately disinterest and failure.

The second criterion is time. As was mentioned previously, thorough research takes time. Comparing the performance of students on a pre-test with later results on a post test might take a full year of school days or at least a semester of attendance. Longitudinal studies comparing students of past years to students of present times could take two years or more. The researcher must consider the question; therefore, "Do I have the time to complete this research?" Or, better yet, "Do I want to spend the time necessary to complete this study?"

Just because the previous two criteria are satisfied, however, doesn't mean the project will be successful. The next criterion, therefore, might be the most important one. This criterion is the <u>availability of supporting research</u>. Although <u>all</u> research is original, some studies are of a "ground-breaking" nature-meaning no research has been done in that area before. While research of this type is laudatory, it is also very difficult.

In this case, the difficulty arises because there is no supporting research from which to draw. Before Pavlov conducted his research on the effects of operant conditioning, no other researcher entered this field. Practically everything Pavlov did, he did from "scratch". Having no previous research to draw upon, his experiments entailed trial and error. Naturally, it took many years to test and verify his results before he could draw meaningful and accurate conclusions.

Since very few practitioners attempt research that is totally new or "ground-breaking", it is necessary to turn to another type of original research. This is research that is supported by previous literature. In other words, the project manager asks herself "What was done before on this subject and what were the results?" In this manner, the project manager doesn't <u>have</u> to start from ground zero. She doesn't <u>have</u> to work by trial and error—she can learn by the successes and failures of others as listed in the research.

This, then, brings the question—"How original does the research have to be?" As with most research questions, this is not easy to define. Essentially, research must be original to the time and place of the researchers. However, one can "piggyback" on the research of another that has been conducted previously. For example, let's say that a person wants to try a method of teaching reading to a classroom of first grade students in a particular setting. It is entirely permissible for a researcher to try the SAME method with the SAME procedures and the SAME hypotheses on a DIFFERENT group of students in a DIFFERENT setting to see if the SAME results can be achieved. Thus, the researcher has CONTINUED the research of another and INCREASED the body of knowledge in the research literature of that topic. Since the setting and the subjects of the research are different, this can be considered to be original research. Research of this type, naturally, involves a thorough review of the existing literature which will be discussed shortly.

The fourth criterion, then, is the <u>Value to the profession</u>. In other words, how does this research contribute to the existing knowledge in the literature? If research is conducted thoroughly and is done according to the established principles of research methodology, it should contribute to the existing knowledge of that subject no matter how small the project may be.

Finally, one must ask—<u>"What is the value of this research to me in my personal work setting?"</u> Hopefully, the research is not just done for the sake of completing a project or a requirement of some sort. It stands to reason that if one takes the time and effort to do research, it should have a direct benefit to the specific work setting. In other words, the questions might be asked "Will the findings of this study have a positive effect on my teaching?" "Will the results benefit my students, my school or my school district?" "How can my work setting be improved from what it was before?"

Accordingly, then, the topic of study needs to be confined to the conditions under which the researcher has control. For a teacher, the conditions might be her own classroom or those students for which she has control. For a principal, the conditions might be her own school or the grade levels in that school. The superintendent has a wider latitude to study because he or she has the entire school district in which to work. It is of little use to attempt a research project if one does not have the authority or the necessary cooperation of others.

Titling the Project and Finding Resources

By now it must be obvious to the reader that if the scope of the project is limited to the school or classroom then the title of the project must also be limited. Thus a title such as "The Effects of Literature-Based Instructions on Third Grader Readers" is too broad. This title leaves too many factors open to question—"What type of effects are being researched?" "What type of literature-based instruction is being used?" "Who are the students and where are they located?"

An improved and revised title, therefore, would look like this—"The Effects of the Stanford Literature-Based Instruction on the Achievement of Third Grade readers in the John A. Kaufhold Elementary School." Normally, this is about as specific as one might get in Mrs. Smith's class in Charlotte, North Carolina. Specific information such as this would be included in the body of the report. It is important to note, however, that the title of the study must directly relate to the research questions and the subsequent findings. If one begins to research the effects of the literature-based method on ACHIEVEMENT, it is not proper to expand the study to include DISIPLINE BEHAVIORS or other areas that aren't previously denoted. In other words, stick to your point and do not go wandering in different directions without changing your title and research questions.

Sample Research Topics

Some sample research topics are as follows:

1- The Relationship of Reading Achievement and Family Size Among First Grade Students
2- Fifth Grade Students' Mathematics Achievement in Relation to their Teachers' Desire to Teach Mathematics
3- The Relationship Between Teacher Age and Degree of Burnout

4- Gender differences in Mathematics Achievement

5- The Relationship Between Reading Skill and Writing Performance Among High School Students

6- Regular and Special Educators' Attitudes toward Students with Special Needs

7- Occupational Stress of Teachers of Emotionally and Mentally Disabled Students

8- Teacher Burnout Among Public and Private School Teachers

9- Pre-Service Teachers' Attitudes Toward Mainstreaming Students.

10- The Relationship Between Television Habits and Reading Ability Among Fourth Grade Students.

Once the title and the scope of the project are determined it is time to locate the resources. Resources are of three types. There are Preliminary Sources, Primary Sources and Secondary Sources. Preliminary sources are those sources that help the researcher find references. These sources are books, digests, professional journals, abstracts or government publications. In other words, preliminary resources are those that are used to find the sources of information needed to begin research.

After the sources of information are found, it is necessary to distinguish the Primary Sources from the Secondary Sources. Primary sources, simply put, are those materials written by the original author. They may be books, articles, monographs or position papers but they must be written first-hand by the actual author. Sometimes, however, the original writer is no longer living or else his or her language is too technical for the average reader to understand. In this case, it is permissible to consult a Secondary Source.

The Secondary Source is one who writes about the work of the primary source. Often, this writer abbreviates the original work or "translates" it into more readable language. Thus, the secondary source is a "reporter" of the first source. An example might be as follows: in order to learn about Progressive Education, one could read Democracy and Education by John Dewey who was the founder of this movement. Dewey's writing is rather tedious to read, however, and it might be easier to refer to a textbook on educational psychology in order to learn about Dewey's method. In this example, Dewey's book, Democracy in Education would be the primary source while the textbook would be the secondary source.

Each type of reference has its advantage. The primary source is true, accurate and unaltered but it may be outdated or difficult to read. The secondary source is capsulized and clearly explained, but some meaning may have been distorted by the writer or some important information may have been omitted. Generally speaking, wherever possible it is advisable to use the primary source first and supplement it with the secondary reference.

Preliminary Sources

Popular preliminary sources might be library books or textbooks by the original author. While the advantage of this reference is accuracy, the disadvantage is timeliness. In many cases, the time between the author's writing the book and the time it appears in print could be two or three years. The possibility exists, therefore, that in some fields more up-to-date information is available in other resources.

The Current Index to Journals in Education, (CIJE) is published monthly and lists articles appearing in numerous journals on all kinds of educational topics. The researcher can use the CIJE to get an overview of topics and then locate journal articles on a particular subject. A second valuable index is the Education Index. This is an electronic index of articles published in educational periodicals since 1983. this provides bibliographic information and abstracts of sources pertaining to topics that have been researches. BOTH of these sources are EXCELLENT PLACES to begin research.

Another good source of references are handbooks and journals such as the following:

Adolescence
American Educational Research Journal
American Journal of Mental Deficiency
Child Development
Cognition and Learning
Contemporary Educational Psychology
Counselor Education and Supervision
Developmental Psychology
Education and Urban Society
Educational Administration Quarterly
Educational Research Quarterly
Health Education
Journal of Agricultural Education
Journal of Counseling Psychology
Journal of Educational Administration
Journal of Educational Psychology
Journal of Educational Research
Journal of Experimental Education
Journal of Learning Disabilities
Journal of Marital and Family Therapy
Journal of Personnel Evaluation in Education
Journal of Research in Childhood Education
Journal of Research in Science Teaching
Journal of Special Education
Journal of Speech and Hearing Disorders
Journal of Teacher Education
Journal of Teaching in Physical Education
Journal of Vocational Behavior
Peabody Journal of Education
Psychology in the Schools

Reading Research Quarterly

Research in Rural Education

Review of Educational Research

Computer Databases

The electronic catalog found in the library is an example of a database. This is nothing more than a collection of units maintained on a computer. Computer databases are available at most university and public libraries. A list of computer databases follows:

Educational Resources Information Center—(ERIC)

This is the world's largest databases on education. It was established in 1966 by the National Library of Education as part of the United States Department of Education's Office of Educational Research and Improvement. The online database provides information on subjects ranging from early childhood and elementary education to education for gifted children and students with disabilities.

ERIC is used by more than 500,000 people each year and contains access to over a million bibliographic citations. In 2004, the Web site was updated by the U.S. Department of Education. Because of its quick, user-friendly features, ERIC is a good preliminary source and a good starting point for research. Additional abstracts are as follows:

Dissertation Abstracts. Dissertation Abstracts contains bibliographic citations and abstracts from all subject areas for doctoral dissertations and master's theses completed at more than 1,000 accredited colleges and universities worldwide. The database dates back to 1861, with abstracts included from 1980 forward. If after reading an abstract you wish to obtain a copy of the complete dissertation, check to see if it is available in your library. If not, speak to a librarian about how to obtain a copy. The results of a Dissertation Abstracts search are shown in Figure 1

Readers' Guide to Periodical Literature. Readers' Guide to Periodical Literature is an index similar in format to the Education Index. Instead of professional publications, however, it indexes articles in nearly 200 widely read magazines. Articles located through the Readers' Guide will generally be nontechnical, opinion-type references. These can be useful in documenting the significance of your problem. The Readers' Guide lists bibliographic information for each entry. To obtain an article listed in the Readers' Guide, search your library's catalog for the magazine in which the article appears. If your library holds that magazine, it will be located in the periodicals department.

Annual Review of Psychology. The Annual Review of Psychology includes reviews of psychological research that are often relevant to educational research. It provides bibliographic information and abstracts for such specific areas as child development, educational administration, exceptional child education, and language teaching.

The internet and the World Wide Web also provide information and resources in education. In a matter of seconds the researcher can access thousands (sometimes tens of thousands) of full-text articles, bibliographic information and abstracts. It is also possible to access up-to-the minute research reports.

While the advantages with this type of research lies with quickness and a wide range of information, there are some limitations. In the first place, many of the articles do not list the author's name or affiliation. This places the researcher in the awkward position of accepting information from an UNKNOWN source. Secondly, even if the writer's name is listed, it is difficult to determine if that person is an AUTHORITY on the subject. Finally, there is no way of knowing if the article is from a REFEREED journal. When a journal is listed as a refereed publication, it means that a panel of experts have examined the articles for validity and reliability before they are published. This ensures that any data or information presented have passed the scrutiny of acceptable research procedures.

When using information from any sources on the World Wide Web, therefore, the researcher should apply the principles of a "healthy skepticism" discussed in chapter one—"Who is the author? Why are they writing the article? What is their affiliation? When was the article written?

{Note: The use of the criteria just listed cannot be over-emphasized! On a personal note, I once had a student present information from a harmless-sounding website. Upon further investigation, it turned out to be from a Satanic web page!}

Following are some Websites that are particularly useful to educational researchers. In addition, electronic indexing and abstract sources can be accessed by utilizing search engines such as Yahoo, Excite, Infoseek, or Lycos. Addresses containing "ed" or ending in "edu" are related to educational institutions while those ending in ".com" are from commercial enterprises.

Uncover Periodical Index (http://www.unm.edu/-brosen/uncover.htm). Uncover is a database with brief descriptive information about articles from more than 17,000 multidisciplinary journals. If you register (for a fee) with Uncover REVEAL, an automated alerting service, you will receive monthly tables of contents from your favorite periodicals. The service also allows you to create search strategies for your research topics.

NewJour (http://gort.ucsd.edu/newjour/). This site provides an up-to-date lists of journals and newsletters available on the Internet on any subject. Using NewJour's search option, you can do a title search to see if a specific journal is currently on the Web, or do a subject search to find out which journals in a particular subject are available on the Internet. Direct links are provided to available journals.

Education Week (http://www.edweek.org/). Full-text articles from *Education Week,* a periodical devoted to education reform, schools, and policy, are available at the site. In addition to current and past articles, the site provides background data to enhance current news, resources for teachers, and recommended Web sites to investigate for other information.

Journal of Statistics Education (http://www.amstat.org/publications/jse/). This electronic journal provides abstracts and full-text articles that have appeared since 1993. interesting features of the journal are "Teaching Bits: A Resource for Teachers of Statistics" and "Datasets and Stories."

CSTEEP. The Center for the Study of Testing, Evaluation, and Educational Policy (http://www.csteep.bc.edu/). The Web site for this educational research organization contains information on testing, evaluation, and public policy studies on school assessment practices and international comparative research.

National Center for Education Statistics (http://www.nces.ed.gov/). This site contains statistical reports and other information on the condition of U.S. education. It also reports on education activities internationally.

Developing Educational Standards (http://www.edstandards.org/Standards.html). This site contains a wealth of up-to-date information regarding educational standards and curriculum frameworks from all sources (national, state, local, and other). Information on standards and frameworks can be linked to by subject area, state, governmental agency, or organization. Entire standards and frameworks are available.

Internet Resources for Special Education (http://specialed.miningco.com). This site provides links to a variety of topics, including reaching resources for regular education and special education teachers; Web sites for students to visit; disability information, resources, and research; disability laws; special education laws; assistive technology; clearinghouses; and information about current topics of interest.

U.S. Department of Education (http://www.ed.gov/). This site contains links to the U.S. government's education databases (including ERIC). It also makes available full-text reports on current findings on education. In addition, it provides links to research offices and organizations, as well as research publications and products. One Department of Education publication, *A Researcher's Guide to the Department of Education*, helps researchers access the various resources that the department has to offer.

Developing Research Questions or Hypotheses

When the topic is narrowed and the initial research is completed, it is time to get to the fine points of the study. It is now when the researcher asks herself, "EXACTLY what do I want to find out about my topic?" This is done by posing research questions or by stating hypotheses. It is not necessary to do both.

Research questions should be succinct and to the point. They need not be lengthy or verbose. Anyone reading the research report from laymen to professional educators should clearly understand what is meant by the research questions. Additionally, these questions lay the foundation for surveys or questionnaires used to collect data.

For example, let's examine possible research questions for a previously mentioned study—Regular and Special Education Teachers' Attitudes Toward Students With Special Needs. Sample research questions here might be:

1- Do teachers in the regular classroom believe that students with special needs benefit from being in the regular classroom?

2- Does the regular classroom teacher believe that regular instruction is altered by the inclusion of children with disabilities?

3- To what degree does the regular classroom student benefit from association with students with special needs?

4- How are the social patterns of the classroom affected by the inclusion of special needs students?

Questions 5-8 would then be repeated for the special education teacher

It is important to note here that questions must be stated in a NEUTRAL fashion to eliminate any signs of bias of "expected" results. For example, a question such as

"Does the regular classroom teacher believe that regular instruction is disrupted by the inclusion of children with disabilities?

denotes some pre-determined bias and an "expected" result. In legal parlance, this might be akin to "leading the witness".

Properly designed survey questions (discussed in the next chapter) should provide data to answer the research questions if they are presented to an equal number of regular classroom teachers and special education teachers in an adequate sample. The research questions do not have to be presented in a large number (depending on the project) but they should be sufficient to yield the necessary data.

Using Hypotheses

There are times, however, when the researcher chooses NOT to take a neutral stance in the supposition of research results. In this case, he will state a hypothesis. The hypothesis is simply a statement that the researcher makes prior to beginning a project in which he or she reveals the results that the project is expected to produce. It is a prediction (one would say an "educated guess") of the research findings.

There are three general types of hypotheses. These are: a directional hypothesis, a non-directional hypothesis and a null hypothesis. The directional hypothesis, simply put, states the direction that the results will follow. This usually means that one group of scores will be higher or that there will be an increase or decrease in the dependent variable. Often, a level of statistical significance is included.

The non-directional hypothesis states that there will be an expected change in the dependent variable but it does not speculate just how that change will occur. This hypothesis might note that there will be a statistically different change in the variable as caused by the independent variable but no direction is attached to the change.

The last type of hypothesis is the null hypothesis. The null hypothesis states that there will be no significant relationship of difference between variables. This type of hypothesis is only used when there is little research or support for the hypothesis. Statistical tests for the null hypothesis are usually more conservative than they are for directional hypotheses. Since few studies are actually designed to verify the non-existence of a relationship, most studies use either the directional or non-directional approach.

Whatever type of hypothesis is used, a good hypothesis should meet all of the following criteria:

1- It is based on sound reasoning that is based on theory or previous research.
2- It presents a concise and clear expectation of the predicted outcome.
3- It clearly states the expected relationship between the defined variables.
4- It is testable and able to be proved.

Using one of the research topics from chapter one, a hypothesis of each type will be developed to fit the study. The study used will be: Fifth Grade Students' Mathematics Achievement in Relation to their Teachers' Desire to Teach Mathematics.

Directional Hypothesis-

"Fifth grade students whose teachers desire to teach mathematics will score significantly higher on an EOG test than those students whose teachers do no desire to teach mathematics."

Non-Directional Hypothesis-

"There will be a significant difference in the EOG scores of fifth grade students whose teachers desire to teach mathematics and those whose teachers do not desire to teach mathematics."

Null Hypothesis

"There will be no significant difference in the EOG scores of fifth grade students whose teachers desire to teach mathematics and those whose teachers do not desire to teach mathematics"

As with the use of research questions, more than one hypothesis can be used in order to determine the amount of information that the researcher needs to know.

Many beginning researchers have the misconception that if their hypotheses are proven false then their projects are a failure. This is not true. In research, it is just as valuable to know what isn't supportable by data as it is to know what is supportable. Either way, the findings contribute to the body of research literature and to the expansion of the knowledge base.

Summary

This chapter demonstrated how research topics are selected and organized. Information was presented on choosing a topic, finding resources and arranging the study. Information was presented on developing research questions and stating hypotheses. The next chapter deals with methods of collecting data and using it to answer research questions.

Chapter 3

How Data Are Collected And Used

ARE? Yes, ARE. You see, the word "data" is plural-meaning "more than one". Thus, the word "data" always requires the plural usage. Data collection procedures are numerous. Data can be collected by a survey, a questionnaire, an interview or an observation. In many cases, a combination of these methods is used. Each of these procedures will be discussed at length.

The Survey

The survey is the most popular way to collect data. It is quick, relatively easy and it can reach a large number of people. If done properly, the survey can yield a good amount of data in a short period of time. The survey presents numerical data that can be arranged and analyzed quickly and accurately if the proper statistical procedures and formulas are applied.

While this method is a very sound way to collect data, it is not without its drawbacks. One obvious limitation is the cost of reproducing the survey and the mailing costs for sending and receiving it. One must remember to include a return addressed stamped envelope for the recipients. Although the survey can yield a large amount of data, this data often lacks depth. Since most of the survey questions require a one-word answer or a checkmark in a box, there is little opportunity for the participant to elaborate of his or her response. A survey that is poorly designed can also produce false or misleading data if the questions are vague or if they lean toward a bias.

Finally, there are other considerations to keep in mind when collecting data from a survey. For instance, did the person for whom the survey was intended actually complete the questions? (a busy superintendent or principal might have given the survey to a subordinate to complete). Next, how much time did the person take to complete the survey? (again, a busy person might go down the list of items and check off answers with little or no thought). A very important consideration that is critical to the use of the data is the question—are the answers truthful? (a superintendent, principal or teacher might be reluctant to show his or her school in a bad light).

All of these limitations can be overcome with proper care and planning but they are shown in order to illustrate that data should not just be accepted at face value without scrutiny. Some ways to overcome these disadvantages are as follows:

1- Fields test the survey with a controlled sample to test for validity and reliability (to be discussed later).
2- Revise questions that prove to be vague, misleading or biased.
3- Allow for privacy and anonymity of respondents.
4- Build in "check questions" to cover previous responses.
5- Allow several lines for additional written comments.

Construction of the Survey

The first step in building a good survey is to return to the research questions or the hypotheses and ascertain what type of information is needed in order to answer the questions. Each question on the survey should be pointed toward the hypotheses. Next, it is wise to consider the length of the survey—how much time will it take to complete? Place yourself in the position of the respondent—would you voluntarily spend 15 minutes of your time of your time completing a survey for someone you don't know? Probably not. A good rule of thumb for determining the length of the survey is that it should be long enough to answer the research questions but short enough to ensure completion. Depending on the subject, 15-30 questions should suffice.

Most surveys employ the use of a Likert scale. This is simply a scale (usually 1-5) asking the reader to rank his or her responses from low to high. In some cases, words such as "always" "sometimes" "seldom" are used. Care must be taken, however, in order to avoid ambiguity. For example, "mostly" and "sometimes" are too close to discriminate as are "seldom" and "hardly ever".

Finally, the survey should make a neat appearance and should not contain any spelling or grammatical errors. Questions should not be overlong and, if possible, should all be on the same page. If it is desirable, there should also be a place on the survey for the participant to include their position, gender, years of service and any other information that may prove useful later on.

The Questionnaire

At the risk of stating the obvious, the questionnaire and the survey are nearly alike with the exception that the questionnaire is usually comprised of short questions that can be answered by a yes/no response. Because of the brevity of the questions, the researcher could possibly ask twice as many questions than would normally be asked on a survey. In some instances, an open-ended one or two word reply would be solicited. At any rate, the SAME DIRECTIONS AND PRECAUTIONS APPLY to the construction and use of the questionnaire as with the construction and use of the survey.

The Cover Letter and the Follow-Up Letter

When using a survey or a questionnaire, it is good protocol to use a cover letter. The letter should be brief, professional and, whenever possible, addressed to the specific person. Tactically speaking, the cover letter can "make or break" the researcher's survey. Here are some important points to include:

1- Explain the purpose of the study-emphasizing the importance and the significance of the project.

2- Give the respondents a good reason for cooperating. Explain how THEY will benefit from the research or how it will improve the educational process. (Note: saying that you need the data to complete a thesis or a dissertation is NOT a good enough justification)/

3- Include a willingness to share the results of the study when it is completed.

4- Include your affiliation with the college or university along with assurances that the study has been approved by the officials in charge.

5- Inform the respondent of the measures taken to ensure anonymity for the respondents.

6- Give the respondents a specific date or deadline by which to return the completed questionnaire or survey.

Ideally, all respondents will return the survey on time but this is seldom the case. Some surveys might get lost, stolen or eaten by the dog or some people just might forget to return them. In this case, the researcher needs to send another survey to the non-respondents along with a polite reminder letter. In order to do this, the researcher needs to pre-code all of the surveys in order to identify who has returned the survey and who has not. Usually, those who are genuinely interested in your study will respond to this polite nudge.

The Interview

Data can also be collected by the use of a personal interview. This technique has several advantages over the survey. A face-to-face interview can give the research the opportunity to ask in-depth or probing questions that will yield additional information. In some instances, people might "open-up" more in a private interview than they would on paper. Further, because of the personal contact, the researcher can tell the emotions that are associated with the response. This approach makes it easier to see if the respondent is avoiding the issue or giving a pat or safe answer. In addition, the chances of vagueness or ambiguity are lessoned in an interview because the interviewer can always call for clarity in order to clear up any misunderstandings. A final advantage of the interview, of course, is that there is immediate feedback. The researcher doesn't have to wait for responses to be sent back in the mail.

Two great disadvantages of this technique are time and money. It takes quite a bit of time to conduct a good interview (20-30 minutes) and, because the interview is face-to-face, one must travel to the site of the interviewee. Because of these two factors, a third difficulty arises—the number of subjects interviewed is relatively small when compared to the numbers reached by a survey.

As in the survey, questions are asked in the interview that are directly related to the hypotheses. Unlike the survey, skill is needed on the part of the interviewer in order to retrieve the necessary data from the participant. If the interviewer is too anxious or overbearing, the respondent could "freeze up" and the information given might be shallow or inconsequential. On the other hand, the respondent might be too eager and might give answers that he or she thinks the interviewer wants to hear. The skill that comes into play here is the ability to sort out the relevant data from the irrelevant Subjectivity has a way of entering into the interview process. The interviewer may read a person as being aloof when she is merely shy. Or a person might be considered to be evasive when he is just cautious. Also, care must be given to be impassive to responses given. Signs of approval, shock or disapproval must be avoided. Finally, it may be difficult to obtain information of a sensitive nature in a face-to-face interview. Some people might not feel comfortable discussing subjects such as race relations or financial matters in person.

Some points for conduction a successful interview are as follows:

1- Be a good listener, don't interrupt, let the person talk.
2- Stay on track. You may have to gently guide the subject back to the topic.
3- Don't "lead the witness," remain impartial.
4- Don't be afraid to probe deeper if necessary or to ask for clarification.
5- Maintain eye contact as much as possible.

Other good suggestions for a successful interview are to arrive on time and to stick to the allotted time period. This is merely a courtesy to the interviewee recognizing that his or her time is just as valuable as yours. A comfortable, private setting should be selected for the meeting-one that is free from noise or interruptions. It is usually advisable to ask the person if he or she minds if you take notes or if you record the conversation.

If these procedures are met and the interviewer is well prepared, the interview should be successful. Confidentiality of responses should be kept and assurances given to the participant that all information will be kept private (it might be best to make this statement at the beginning of the interview and repeat it at the end). As with the survey, offer to share the results of the research at the conclusion of the study.

Despite the increased difficulties that the interview method presents, it is an excellent way of gathering truthful, relevant data. In this instance, the research "tool" is the interviewer and not the survey instrument. Because of this, the "tool" can be changed and improvised to accommodate the person and the situation.

The Observation

Perhaps the least used form of data collection is the observation. While it is definitely experimental and it yields empirical evidence, the observation method can, nevertheless, be tricky. There are several reasons for this statement and they can best be presented in terms of precautions. First, the statement that "everything is not always as it seems" can be true when applied to an observation. A scene of classroom behavior, for example, may not be the same on one day as it is on the next.

Secondly, due to a phenomenon known as "observer effect", the subjects observed may behave differently under observation than they would normally. A classroom full of children, for example, may be on their best behavior when a "visitor" is in the room. Or, conversely, they might be overly excited and "act out" when someone new is in their environment. Any behavior out of the ordinary would, of course, distort the data.

Thirdly, the danger of observer bias is most prevalent in this type of data collection. What appears to be disruptive noise or horseplay to one observer may be considered to be enthusiasm or "working noise" to another. This type of data collection calls for a lot of restraint and objectivity on the part of the observer. Personal feelings, attitudes and prejudices must be laid aside in the name of objective, scientific recording of events.

Fortunately, there are ways to overcome these three deficiencies just mentioned. One observation doesn't make an accurate report. Therefore, it takes several observations at different times of the day and week to ascertain the true demonstration of a group's behavior. It is difficult to pinpoint the exact number of observations that are needed but, sooner or later, the researcher will get a "feel" for what constitutes normality in the behavior of the group.

These repeated visits in conjunction with an inconspicuous presence will eventually offset the dangers of "observer effect". After awhile, the observer will be considered as just another classroom fixture. After an initial introduction by the teacher and an explanation of the purpose of the visit, the class will generally lose its curiosity about the newcomer.

Observer bias, on the other hand, is harder to control. If the data gathered from the visits can be considered to be valid, reasonable proof must be shown that observer bias was eliminated. One way this proof can be shown is to construct rubrics of behavior observed. In other words, what sort of behaviors exemplify something such as "time on task"? What behaviors illustrate "good discipline" or "respect for others"? Once these behaviors are established in a pre-determined rubric or checklist, it is easier to justify the recorded data.

The best way to offset observer bias, however, is the use of a technique known as triangulation. This is where there are two or more observers who are trained to watch for the behaviors listed on the rubric. When the data are gathered, comparisons are made of the data collected by each observer. A simple test of inter-rater reliability can be made by either "eye-balling" the results or by applying a reliability formula (discussed later).

Once the inter-rater reliability has been established, the data stand a good chance of being accurate and valid. Two other considerations must be made in determining the validity of data. These considerations involve the factors of high inference observation or low inference observation. In a low inference observation, the researcher merely records what is seen. For example, how many times does Harry disrupt the class? How many minutes does the teacher talk while students sit passively and listen? How many questions does the teacher ask during the lesson? In recording these instances, no judgments or inferences are necessary. Only factual information is recorded here.

With high inference observations, the opposite is true. Judgments and inferences are essential to this report. Thus, the observer notes what CAUSES Harry to disrupt the class, what precipitates his actions? What are the consequences of his behavior? Now, instead of just recording the number of questions asked by the teacher, the observer notes the TYPES of questions. Are they one answer questions? Are they thought-provoking question? How does the teacher respond to the answers given? Generally speaking, a good and true observation will include BOTH the high inference and the low inference recordings.

To complete the observation process, items of standard protocol are shown below:

- Who is being observed? How many people are involved, who are they, and what individual roles and mannerisms are evident?
- What is going on? What is the nature of the conversation? What are people saying or doing?
- What is the physical setting like? How are people seated, and where? How do the participants interact with each other?
- What is the status or roles of a person; who leads, who follows, who is decisive, who is not? What is the tone of the session? What beliefs, attitudes, values, and so on, seem to emerge?
- How did the meeting end? Was the group divided, united, upset, bored, or relieved?
- What activities or interactions seemed unusual or significant?
- What was the observer doing during the session? What was the observer's level of participation in the observation (participant observer, nonparticipant observer, etc.)?

Sampling Technique

Sampling is the process of selecting a number of participants for a study that will represent the population from which they were selected. This, a sample is comprised of persons, items or events that make up a larger group. Since educational research deals most often with students, the subject of samples will be discussed in terms of people. Five different types of sampling will be discussed: Random, Systematic, Stratified, Cluster and Volunteer.

Random Sampling

Random sampling is the process of selecting a sample in such a way that all individuals in the defined population have an equal and independent chance of being selected for the sample (Gay, Mills, Airasian 2006). In this case, every individual in the defined population has as equal chance of being selected. The selection process is completely out of the researcher's control. Random sampling is a highly accurate way of obtaining a representative sample and, for this reason; it is most often used on various methods of research.

Stratified Sampling

A second, highly efficient method on conduction sampling is to use a stratified sample. In using this technique, the target population is divided into subgroups that comprise the whole. Each subgroup is represented in proportion to which they exist in the population. For example, if the target population of a school district consists of 60% whites, 25% African-Americans, 15% Hispanic or Latino and 10% Asian, then the sample must reflect the same percentages. These subgroups can then be broken down further in terms of gender, age, socio-economic level, etc. as long as they are represented in the same proportion as the target population. NOTE: While highly accurate, this type of sampling may require a great deal of time and effort on the part of the researcher.

Systematic Sampling

Systematic sampling is relatively simple and easy to use because it is drawn from a controlled population on a list. Each member of the sample is chosen by a procedure. In many instances, this procedure is just to use every fifth name or every tenth name-depending on the size of the population.

While this type of sampling has a degree of randomness, it can evoke a degree of bias in the event that certain nationalities in the population have distinctive last names that tend to be grouped together under certain letters of the alphabet (Irish-O'Brian, O'Toole, etc. Scottish—MacDonald, MacKenzie, etc.) taking every fifth name from a population such as this could possible distort the sample. Using a population list that is alphabetized could also distort the sample because the surnames beginning with the letters Q, U, X, and Z are few in number.

Cluster Sampling

A type of sampling frequently used for collecting educational data is cluster sampling: this type of sampling is popular and useful since intact groups—not individuals—are randomly selected. These "intact" groups usually consist of students in a particular grade level. For example, in a study concerned with dropout prevention, the researcher could study ninth grade students in one or more schools and generalize the results to the entire ninth grade population of the school district.

Volunteer Sampling

A convenient but less reliable type of sampling is volunteer sampling. The difficulty with this type of sampling is that it lacks random selection since not all of the members of a group choose to volunteer. In addition, there is the possibility that volunteer subjects may introduce bias into the study-they may have more interest in the study, they may be of higher intelligence or are better educated. Further, they may be motivated by pay (subjects are sometimes paid to participate) or in order to gain recognition or favor in the eyes of the researcher.

The reliability factor is present in this type of sampling, since the research has no way of knowing how people who refuse to participate differ from those who volunteer. Thus, the results cannot be generalized to an entire population.

Avoiding Sample Error and Bias

Even when using the best of sampling techniques, there is no guarantee that the sample will be free of errors. This is the reality of random sampling. No matter how well constructed a sample may be, it can never agree precisely with the composition of the population. This difference is routinely designated as "sampling error." Sampling error can be effectively controlled by further stratification and can be accommodated by statistical formulas that will be presented later.

Sampling bias, on the other hand, can be diagnosed as a distinct fault of the researcher. A study conducted on college students' reaction to a foreign language requirement in the curriculum would show bias if the researcher stood outside of the department of foreign languages and interviewed those students who passed by. Presumably, these students might be foreign language majors who have a preference for this subject. These results could not be generalized to all college students with any degree of validity. Sampling bias can also occur with a low return rate of surveys or questionnaires. A return rate of only thirty or forty percent could detract from the validity of the results.

In some instances, sampling error, sampling bias and a low return rate are beyond the control of the researcher. When this happens, one is forced to just use the data that is received. It this happens, it is the duty of the researcher to include this information in the "limitations" section of the research report in order that the reader can have this information before reading further.

Information concerning the validity of survey results can be subjected to a variety of tests to explain or account for sampling error or bias.

These tests can be built into a research study prior to its inception and thus embarrassing questions asked about the study by readers can effectively be avoided. These tests come under the heading of internal validity and external validity and will be discussed in the next chapter.

Summary

In this chapter, various methods of collecting data were discussed. These methods included the use of surveys, questionnaires, observation techniques and the interview. Advantages and disadvantages of each approach were included as well as techniques for implementation. Finally, different types of procedures were presented for collecting data by sampling. The following chapter will deal with ways to analyze the data collected in order to determine its usefulness to the researcher.

In the precious chapter, we examined ways of gathering data. Before we can use this data, however, we must first see if it is believable and useful. In order to determine this, we must apply the tests of validity and reliability. The first, and most important of the tests is validity.

Chapter 4

Determining Validity and Reliability

Another word for validity is "truth". Are the data and subsequent results that they yield actually true? That is to say, can they be believed and are they free from measurement error? Validity can be divided into five components. These types of validity are content, predictive, concurrent, construct and, finally, face validity.

Content Validity

Content validity can be defined as "the degree to which the items on a test represent the content that was taught." Another way to say this is, "Does the test measure what it is supposed to measure?" Theoretically speaking, material is taught to students over a period of time and then an examination is constructed that consists of a series of questions representing an overview of the subject matter in proportion to the time spent teaching each portion. In other words, if a literature teacher spends a week teaching Shakespeare and one day teaching Chaucer, one would logically expect that there would be more questions in the exam on Shakespeare that Chaucer.

Unfortunately, this bit of logic often goes unnoticed by teachers who include a number of disproportionate items in their test. This situation can lead the student who did poorly on the exam to complain that he "studied the wrong material" when, in actuality, it was the teacher's fault for "testing the wrong material."

Since the advent of High Stakes Testing, the whole issue of content validity has been turned upside down. In previous years, there was a broad curriculum consisting of subjects such as art, music, physical education, health, science, math, English and history. The content of these subjects was divided into broad curricular objectives which were then broken into instructional objectives that the teacher used to plan her lesson and the subsequent examination. Thus, if the process was done correctly the examination had content validity and the results could be used to discern those students who had learned as well as those students who failed to learn.

With high stakes testing, the process was reversed. A standardized exam was constructed at the state level which was designed to measure what the students were <u>supposed</u> to learn. Unfortunately, with a discrepancy in teachers' abilities, teachers' instructional methods, a lack of a standardized directional plan and a differentiation of instructional facilities, student scores on these standardized exams varied with dire consequences dealt to schools and school districts whose students scored poorly.

In order to avoid these consequences which often included loss of funding for school districts or loss of jobs for superintendents, principals or teachers, a practice of "teaching for the test" gained popularity. Thus, the content of the curriculum was reduced to the content of the test and any material not thought to be on the test was not taught. Since some schools and some teachers were more assiduous in teaching toward the test through fear or a desire to be competitive (or both) there was a wide discrepancy of test results. Since the initial question of "did the test measure what was taught?" could not be answered conclusively, the test results were not CONCLUSIVELY VALID.

Predictive Validity

Predictive validity is the degree to which the predictions made by a test are confirmed by the later behavior of students. One example of this type of validity can be illustrated by the use of a pre-algebra test given to eighth grade students at the end of the school year to determine their readiness and their aptitude for enrolling in ninth grade algebra. If the scores on the pre-test are positively correlated to the students' performance in ninth grade algebra, it can be said that the pre-test is an adequate predictor of future performance in algebra. Statistically speaking, a high positive correlation would be between .70 and 1.00 (these correlational statistics will be discussed in a later chapter).

Most tests measuring aptitude require a high positive correlation in order to produce predictive validity. Interestingly, the most common aptitude test used for predicting future college success is the Scholastic Aptitude Test (S.A.T.) given to high school students. While this test (or variations thereof) has been used by college admissions offices for decades in an effort to sort those students who are accepted into college from those who are not, the test, itself, has only a moderate predictive validity level of .60!

Concurrent Validity

Concurrent validity is the degree to which scores on one test correlate to the scores on a similar test with the same content. This type of validity is often applied to a new or different type of test which is used to replace an existing test. Using the example just related concerning the S.A.T. examination, when a new form of the S.A.T. is issued, scores on both tests (by the same sample group of students) must be correlated to see if the degree of difficulty is the same.

A classroom application of concurrent validity can be applied when an instructor desires to produce a "make-up" test. Fearing that students may reveal answers to other students, she might construct a new test using the old material. If the results produced by each test can be shown to produce a positive correlation, concurrent validity would be assured.

Construct Validity

Construct validity can be difficult to prove and difficult to measure. This is because construct validity is the extent to which a test can be shown to measure a hypothetical or abstract concept such as creativity, artistic ability or personality. In order to measure these intangible concepts, a type of rubric must be designed and then applied to an individual's later performance.

For instance, how is a candidate for an art school tested for artistic ability? A rubric or measurement device must be determined and then qualitatively gauged with performance. Since statistics cannot generally be applied to these abstract concepts, other measures need to be devised.

Face Validity

A final form of validity (and perhaps the most unusual one) is face validity. Face validity is the extent to which a test APPEARS to measure what it is supposed to measure. This type of validity is important if the students are to take the test seriously and give it their proper attention. A good example to present might be the use of the Rorschak Psychological Test-popularly known as the "ink blot" test. Although this test has been validated and used by psychologists for many years, there are many jokes told about what the ink blots reveal. If a subject, therefore, believed the jokes and, thus (to him), the test lacked face validity, he would not take the test seriously and the ensuing results would be invalid.

Although teachers do not use Rorschak tests, care should be exercised that the tests that they do give will be taken seriously and that the students will give it their best attention. Tests that are poorly typed, laden with spelling errors or include over-long, vague questions may lack face validity and could detract from the students' performance.

Test Reliability

Test reliability is concerned with two important words-DEPENDABILITY AND CONSISTENCY. Questions to ask here are "Can I depend on the testing instrument to consistently measure the same things?" "With all other factors and practices being the same, will I get approximately the same results the next time?" Reliability should not be confused with validity, validity deals with the subject of truth and reliability does not. A testing instrument can be reliably bad—one could depend on it to consistently give improper results.

Thus, reliability can go both ways—reliably correct or reliably incorrect. If a test is VALID, it has to be RELIABLE (reliably good). But, just because a test is reliable doesn't mean its valid. Reliability can be used in three forms: Split-half, Alternate form (also called equivalent or parallel form) and test-retest.

Split Half

Reliability can be judged by splitting a group in half and giving one half the odd numbered questions and the other half the even numbered items. A reliability correlation is then taken to determine if the results are reliable. Split-half reliability is used when it is difficult to get the same participants or similar participants together.

For example, suppose a college professor wants to measure the results of an examination for reliability but, because of scheduling, the course is not taught every semester. Rather than wait a year when the course is taught again, the professor could split the group in two and correlate the scores for reliability.

Alternate Form

In some instances, such as a make-up examination, a different form of a test can be used. This alternate test would contain similar questions drawn from the same content and the same objectives. After administering the test to the same group of participants or to similar group, the scores would be correlated to determine reliability.

Test-retest

Test-retest is a simple way to measure reliability when content knowledge is not required. One example would be a readiness test for reading or math. The test could be administered on one day and re-administered a few weeks later at which time a correlation could be measured between the scores. The difficulty with this method lies in determining the time differential between the tests. An interval of time that is too long or too short could invalidate the results. The proper time period used must be determined by the one who gives the test.

In many instances, the test-retest method is used in physical testing or chemical testing. A test in physical education could be used from one day to the next to determine reliability. A chemical test, such as a blood test, could also be used in the same manner in order to compare the results.

Inter-rater Reliability

With the previously mentioned types of reliability, quantitative data were used. Sometimes, however, qualitative measures are used such as in an observation or a case study. In these cases, it is wise to use two or more raters to ensure that bias is eliminated. In order to do this, each rater's score of the same action or subject is correlated with the other raters' scores to determine if they are consistent and therefore reliable.

Reliability Coefficients

Generally speaking, the larger the number of test items, the better the chance is that reliability can be determined accurately. Thus a test of 100 items would have a better chance of yielding correct reliability than a short test of only 15 items. Consistency of measurement generally increases when the number of test items is also increased.

As with the scores of correlation discussed previously, the scores of reliability are also judged against a perfect 1.00 score. Thus, the closer the reliability coefficient is to 1.00, the better it is. Most standardized tests, for example, usually have a reliability coefficient of .90. Teacher made tests and projective-type tests often have a lower reliability coefficient due to factors of subjectivity.

Formulas for finding the correlation coefficient for reliability are the Kuder Richardson and the Chronbach Alpha. The Kuder Richardson formula is used if there are only two choices per test item (such as a True/ False test) and the Chronbach Alpha is used if there are more choices (such as a multiple choice test or a five point Likert scale). Since both of these formulas can be difficult to compute, Kuder Richardson provided an alternate formula that is easier. This formula takes less time but is also somewhat less reliable. This formula is called the Kuder-Richardson 21 and is as follows:

$$r \text{ (reliability)} = \frac{(K)(SD^2) - M(K-M)}{(SD^2)(K-1)}$$

Where-

K= the number of items in the test

SD= the standard deviation of the scores

M= the mean of the scores

The Standard Error of Measurement

Reliability can also be expressed by the standard error of measurement. This is an estimate of the variance of test scores over a period of time. for instance, if a test was perfectly reliable (no test is) the person's test score would be the same every time (could you imagine getting the same SAT score with every application?) If this were to happen, however, that score would be called the TRUE score. But since this is not probable, each test result would yield a score that varies a few points one way or another. The standard error of measurement, therefore, indicates how much that variance would be. Naturally, the lower the standard error of measurement score, the more reliable a test would be. In this instance, the terms "low" and "high" would be relevant to the number of items on the test. A standard error of 5 would be large on a twenty item test but small for a test of 200 questions.

The formula for the standard error of measurement is as follows:

$$SEM = SD \ \sqrt{1-R}$$

Where:

SEM= the standard error of measurement

SD= the standard deviation of the scores

R= the reliability coefficient

The question of validity and reliability does not stop here, however. There are several factors that can alter the validity of scores and these factors will be discussed next. Once these factors are taken into account, measures of central tendency such as the variance and the standard deviation can be applied to prove validity.

Internal and External Validity

The validity of any study is determined by two major factors:

1- The extent to which changes in the dependent variable can be shown as CAUSED SOLEY by the independent variable
2- The extent to which the results of the study can be generalized to other groups

When condition #1 has been met, the study has <u>internal validity</u>. When condition #2 is met, it has <u>external validity</u>.

In many cases, however, the results of a study may be due to outside factors which had nothing to do with the independent variable. These outside factors are called threats to internal validity.

Threats to Internal Validity

There are ten threats to internal validity and any one of these, if not controlled, can invalidate the results of a study, no matter how carefully it is done. These threats are history, maturation, testing, instrumentation, statistical regression, differential selection of subjects, experimental mortality, selection maturation interaction, Hawthorne Effect, John Henry Effect.

1- <u>History</u>—this involves any changes in the students' environment that may have occurred during the period from the pre-test to the post-test and possibly affected the results of a study.

Example—A fourth grade teacher attempts a new approach to teaching reading. She pre-tests the students in the fall and post-tests them in the spring. The results are significantly improved. However, during the same period, the principal instituted a school-wide program called "Book-it" which offered the students a reward of pizza for the number of books read. QUESTION: Were the reading results due to the teacher's new approach or to the principal's new program?

2- Maturation—Maturation involves any biological or psychological changes that could have taken place in the subjects during the period of the study or the experiment.

Example—Primary grade teachers recognize that there is usually a marked change in their students during the school year from August to June. Depending upon the length of time from the pre-test to the post-test, a good question to ask might be, "Were the project results due to the intervention of the independent variable or were they simply caused by maturation of the subjects?"

3- Testing—This factor deals specifically with the elapsed time period between the pre-test and the post-test.

Example—Positive effects of the study could be due to a short period of time between the tests. In this instance, the students could have performed well because they were already familiar with the questions and the answers.

4- Measuring Instruments/Instrumentation—The measuring instruments used or the actual procedures utilized in the use of the measuring instruments could have brought about altered results.

Example—One teacher might administer a test differently than another teacher—possibly allowing more time to finish or providing helpful hints to slower students. Another instance producing skewed results might deem from the fact that the post-test could be easier that the pre-test. If test grading was done subjectively, standards or criteria could differ from teacher to teacher.

5- Statistical Regression—This is an interesting statistical phenomenon that affects high performing students and low performing students in opposite ways. When a post-test is administrated, students in each group will collectively move closer to the mean.

Example—Students who fall above the 85th percentile generally score lower collectively when they are re-tested. Students who fall below the 15th percentile generally score higher collectively with or without the experimental treatment when they are re-tested. This phenomenon can give the IMPRESSION that the experimental treatment caused the results when, in fact, it did not.

6- Differential Selection of Subjects—This situation can occur if members of the experimental group and the control group exhibit differences in the dependent variable prior to the experiment.

Example—Different criteria might be used to select members of the different groups causing a bias to emerge. In the case of just one group, the "volunteer" factor could cause a bias before the experiment begins. Volunteers typically have a desire to please the experimenter and may not be totally objective in the proceedings.

7- Experimental Mortality—Experimental mortality is perhaps the most common error made in research studies and is one that causes the most inaccuracies in results. It is also known as the "Dropout Factor." This deals with the loss of subjects in a study over a period of time. In other words, are the subjects in the study the exact same group or were these additions or subtractions? Any changes in the group can inflict bias into the study and skew the results.

Example—A researcher may want to compare data from a group of students from the fourth grade to the same group who advanced to the fifth grade. From one year to the next, however, the composition of the group may have changed with some students leaving and some new students coming in. This factor could alter the results of the study dramatically depending on the different students.

8- Selection Maturation Interaction—This factor can occur if two groups, on the average, were at different levels of maturation when tested.

Example—Pre-school age children and primary grade children are often in different levels of maturation. Comparing two different groups of these students might yield dubious results-especially if one group has more males than another group.

9- The Hawthorne Effect—This is another common cause of error in research studies that often produces misleading results. Researchers have found over the years that subjects in a study-from adults to children-may exhibit positive results in a study due to the mere fact that they know they are being observed and their results are measured.

Example—A group of sixth grade students might actually try harder to perform well due to the fact that they have been chosen to participate in a new program. Another case might be subjects in a laboratory setting could work harder because they know that they are part of an experiment. Either of these conditions could appreciably alter the results.

10- The John Henry Effect—This is an opposite reaction to the Hawthorne Effect. In this case, the control group-knowing they are not receiving the experimental treatment-could try harder and successfully succeed in outperforming their counterparts in the experimental group.

Threats to External Validity

External validity, it will be remembered, is the degree to which the results of a study can be generalized and applied to persons, settings and times that are DIFFERENT from those in the original study. In other words, just because a project or a study produced good results with one group of subjects under certain conditions, will it produce similar results to a similar group under similar conditions? A study that is conducted well should be able to meet this criteria. [Note: Not all research studies are expected to be generalized by the researcher and this qualifying statement is usually presented at the beginning of their study.]

Two important conditions to consider in producing external validity are population validity and ecological validity.

Population Validity

This factor deals with sampling techniques. In order to ensure population validity, there must be congruency between the sample drawn, the accessible population used and the target population to which the results are generalized. Graphically, it should look like this:

Sample Population

↓

Accessible Population

↓

Target Population

If these arrows are not in a straight line, population validity cannot be achieved.

Example:

Suppose a study is conducted using a new reading program with a group of first grade students. If the study is successful, the researcher would like to apply the results to all of the first grade students in the school district. Since it is too cumbersome to conduct an experiment with all of the first grade students, an accessible population is selected. This population might be the students in one school. From this accessible population, a sample is drawn and the research is conducted. If the sample and the accessible population match the target population demographically, population validity is achieved. Matching criteria may include race, ethnicity, socio-economic features, age, maturity, and experience of teachers as well as a variety of other factors.

Ecological Validity

The second portion leading to external validity is ecological validity. Ecological validity is concerned with the environmental conditions under which a study is conducted.

Example:

Using the previous example, under what conditions was the research conducted? A first grade class of 32 students with one teacher assistant might perform differently than a class with 20 students and one teacher assistant. Once again, if the sample, the accessible population and the target population are congruent, ecological validity will be achieved.

Research Designs

There are many research designs that can be used be researchers to control the threats to internal validity. Three basic designs are presented that are commonly used by practitioners. Other variations of these designs exist, but they are often used in laboratory settings or by researchers doing extensive study.

The research designs shown next are in symbolic form where:

R= random assignment of subjects

0^1= pre-test

0^2 = post-test

X= experimental treatment

Design #1

This design is the best design to control threats to internal and external validity.

GROUP 1 R 0^1 X 0^2

GROUP 2 R 0^1 0^2

Both groups are randomly selected and are given a pre-test. Group 1 receives the experimental treatment and group 2 (the control group) receives no treatment. Both groups are post-tested to see if the results differ. An option here is to reverse the groups and conduct the study again.

GROUP 2 R 0^1 X 0^2

GROUP 1 R 0^1 0^2

If the results of both trials are the same it may be concluded that the results were due to the experimental treatment.

Design #2

Sometimes, the researcher, due to time constraints, may want to eliminate the pre-test. This design would look like this:

GROUP 1 R X 0^2
GROUP 2 R 0^2

This form would not be quite as valid as design #1 but it would still be useful to the practitioner.

Design #3

This form is very expedient but, unfortunately, it does not control threats to internal validity.

0^1 X 0^2

With only one group receiving the experimental treatment, there is no control group with which to make a comparison. This leaves the results open to question.

Certainly, no research design is perfect and no study is ever 100% accurate no matter how carefully it is done. Design #1, however, lends itself well to research statistics and through the application of various statistical formulas can produce results that are accurate to the degree of 95% (.05 level) or 99% (.01 level) which are acceptable in most research studies.

Summary

This chapter concerned the use of assessment measures in order to determine the accuracy and reliability of data collected. Various measures were presented to ensure internal validity as well as external validity. It was demonstrated in this chapter that data that do not pass the tests of validity and reliability can skew the results of a study and cause embarrassment to the researcher. In the next chapter, it will be shown how the use of descriptive statistics can assist the researcher in refining and verifying the data

Chapter 5

Understanding Descriptive Statistics

In the last chapter, it was shown that before data could be used it had to pass the tests of validity and reliability. In this chapter, the use of descriptive statistics will be presented to show the mathematical methods of proving these two tests.

Descriptive Statistics and the Normal Curve

Are you normal? This is a question that we all ask ourselves at one time or another (some people already know the answer). In other words, how do we stack up to the average? To answer that question, we have to figure out, obviously, what exactly is average. This is where descriptive statistics comes in.

Many things by nature are evenly distributed, meaning that there are generally two extremes, highest and lowest, and then a large middle group. In other words, there is a predictable range of numbers that work into a normal distribution or what is known as a normal curve. A normal curve is bell-shaped and will appear as follows:

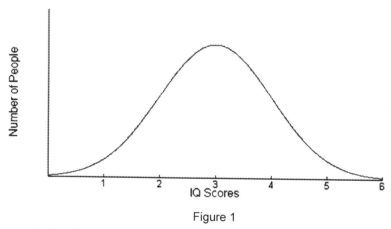

Figure 1

In this illustration the two extremes are shown and the large middle ground is presented. This normal curve represents a normal distribution of virtually all things in nature from the size of trees to the weight of animals to the age and intelligence of humans. Thus, it is the purpose of descriptive statistics to describe quantitatively how a particular characteristic is distributed among a group.

The plotting of a normal curve begins with the construction of a frequency distribution. The frequency distribution is drawn by first showing the extreme numbers and then plotting all of the numbers in between. A frequency distribution of the IQ scores of ten people, therefore, would look like this:

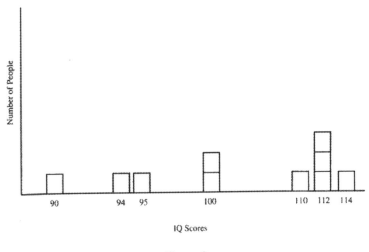

Figure 2

The representative graph shows the number of people with a certain IQ score. If one were to continue to plot the IQ scores of a large group of people from a representative sample of the entire population, the results would appear in the shape of a histogram or a bar graph and, most likely, appear as follows:

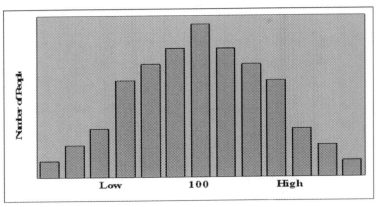

Figure 3

This bar graph would then be translated into a normal curve as illustrated in Figure 1.

Measures of Central Tendency

Once the normal curve is plotted, we can begin to show the measures of central tendency. Central tendency denotes what is average ("are you normal?"), what is above average and what is below average. If the normal curve figure is bisected, it will be noted that 50% of the scores fall to the left of the dividing line and 50% of the scores fall to the right of the line and an exact midpoint is shown. This configuration is imperative in order to represent any normal curve and will appear as illustrated below.

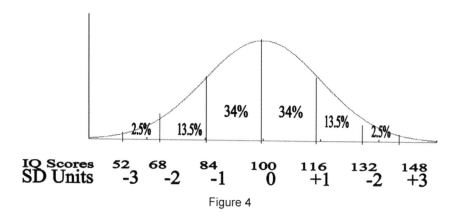

Figure 4

When the normal curve is constructed as shown, it is now possible to construct three measures of central tendency, the MEAN, the MODE and the MEDIAN. The first of these measures is the MEAN. The mean is simply the arithmetic average of the numbers or the scores. Statistically, it is represented like this:

$$M = \frac{\sum x}{N}$$

Where   M= the mean x=Scores

$\sum$= the sum (shown by the Greek letter called Sigma)

N = the number of subjects

So, by using elementary mathematics, the mean or AVERAGE is determined by dividing the number of subjects into the sum of the scores. If the following numbers represent a group of students' scores on a test, the MEAN would be 85.4

SCORES (5)

92

90

85   85.4= 427

81 5

79

427

Figure 5

The next measure of central tendency is the MODE. The mode is simply the most frequently occurring score. In the following set of scores, the mode level would be 79.

SCORES

92

90

85

79→ Mode

79

Figure 6

Another measure of central tendency is called the MEDIAN. This is the exact middle of all the scores; it is the point at which 50% of the scores fall above and 50% of the scores fall below. In the group of an odd number of scores, the median would be 85. The median for an even group of scores would be found by averaging the two middle scores. Thus, the median score for this group would be 86.

Odd Number of Scores (5)	Even Number of Scores (6)
92	92
90	90
85= Median	87} Average = 86
81	85}
79	81
	79

Figure 7.

Statistical Uses of the Mean, Mode, and Median

The statistic given by the mean is important to educational researchers because it presents a picture of what is average. Using the scores in figure 5 a teacher could see how the mean score relates to her grading scale. For example, if the teacher's grading scale was 90%=A, 80%=B, 70%=C, the students' scores would average a B+. The accuracy of this statistic, however, can be thrown off by extreme numbers. Let's say that one student failed to study for a test and recorded a score of only 20. Notice that the mean drops to 71.6 in figure 8.

Scores

92

90

85   $M = \dfrac{358}{5} = 71.6$

81

20

358

Figure 8.

In an era of strict accountability, a low score such as this would negatively distort the mean and would not give a true representation of the pupil's (and the teacher's) performance. In like manner, the use of the mode-as illustrated below—would give a false impression of the students' performance.

Scores
100
100
85
81
79
74

Figure 9

Perhaps, then, the most reliable measure of central tendency is the median since it is the only measure not affected by extremes. It is noteworthy to add, however, that most statistical formulas use the statistic of the mean. This is because that statistic lends itself well to computation (especially if there are no extremes) and is not as cumbersome as the median which necessitates plotting all of the scores to find the exact middle,

Sometimes when using statistics a more accurate picture of central tendency is required. In this case, it is necessary to determine the measures of variability around the mean.

Measures of Variability

To find this degree of variability, it is useful to employ three other measures, the range, the variance and the standard deviation. These will be shown separately.

Range—The range is the distance from the highest scores to the lowest score. In group A below, for example, the range is the distance from score 100 to score 25—a difference of 75 points spread rather equally.

GROUP A 100, 86, 77, 64, 55, 42, 25

This equal spread is not always the case, however, and for this reason the range is not a measure of central tendency. Witness the following example with group. Group B also has a range of 100-25 with a 75 point spread but the scores are not distributed evenly.

GROUP B—100, 50, 45, 38, 25

Thus, while the range is useful for denoting the limits of scores, it is not a good indicator of variability.

Variance—To provide a closer look at the measure of central tendency it is desirable to calculate how far the scores vary from the mean. This measure is called the VARIANCE and shows the average distance from the mean. The variance is calculated by taking the difference between the score and the mean. Notice the variance in the following two examples.

GROUP C		VARIANCE	GROUP D		VARIANCE
SCORES	DIFFERENCE	SCORE (X)	SCORES	DIFFERENCE	SCORE (X)
78	78-75	+3	99	99-75	+24
77	77-75	+2	99	99-75	+24
76	76-75	+1	75	75-75	0
72	72-75	-3	56	56-75	-19
72	72-75	-3	46	46-75	-24
M=75		0	M=75		0

Figure 10

After doing these calculations, however, we still do not have the average distance from the mean. To find the average, after all, we need to add the column and divide by the number of scores. We cannot do this however, because in each case the variance scores (X) total zero. This is normal because the mean is always in the middle and no matter what scores are used, the sum will always be zero.

To get the average distance from the mean, therefore, we need to add an extra step. We need to square the variance scores to get rid of the minus numbers. Thus, the formula for the variance becomes:

$$V = \frac{\sum x^2}{N}$$
the variance equals the sum of X^2 divided by the number of scores.

Using the example in figure 10, the variance would be as follows:

GROUP C

SCORES	DIFFERENCE	VARIANCE SCORES (X)	X^2	
78	78-75	+3	9	Applying the Formula
77	77-75	+2	4	V = 32 = 6.40
76	76-75	+1	1	5
72	72-75	-3	9	
72	72-75	-3	9	
x=75			32	

This figure, 6.40, shows the average distance from the mean (the variance) for this set of scores.

While this calculation was relatively easy for Group C, let's see what happens when we calculate Group D.

GROUP D

SCORES	DIFFERENCE	VARIANCE SCORES (X)	X^2	
99	99-75	+24	576	Applying the Formula
99	99-75	+24	576	V = 2,354 = 470.80
75	75-75	0	0	5
56	56-75	-19	361	
46	46-75	-29	841	
x=75			2,354	

Clearly, this calculation is more cumbersome than the one made for group C and the result is rather vague when applied to the mean of 75. What is needed is an increasingly accurate portrayal of the average distance from the mean. This is accomplished by using the STANDARD DEVIATION.

<u>Standard Deviation</u>

The standard deviation is the most common measure of variability used in statistics. It represents a close approximation of how each score differs from the mean. In other words, it defines what is normal and what are the equal measurements above and below normal. A basic formula for the standard deviation is :

$$SD = \sqrt{\frac{\mathring{a} x^2}{N}}$$

The Greek letter sigma δ is often used to denote standard deviation although the symbol SD is also used. Thus, the standard deviation is nothing more than the SQUARE ROOT of the VARIANCE. Applying this formula to the data for each group yields the following scores.

Group C	Group D
SD = square root of 6.40 = 2.53	SD= square root of 470.80 = 21.70

This shows that although each group has identical means, the scores of group D show a much wider variance. Generally speaking, a wide variance of 21 points on a mean of 75 would indicate a broad discrepancy in the students' performance—a possible indicator that there might be a placement error in assigning the group.

To illustrate a practical application of the standard deviation, the reader must return to figure 4. Two popular measures of human intelligence were recorded in data used for the Stanford-Binet IQ test and the Wechsler IQ test. Both tests yielded a normal distribution of scores from a representative sample of the total population. The normal curve in figure 4 shows a mean of 100-one hundred being the score for average intelligence. One half of the sample tested scored above 100 and one half scored below this figure. But, precisely HOW MUCH ABOVE and HOW MUCH BELOW? This is what we want to know. For this we need to use the standard deviation.

Applying the formula for standard deviation to this data the researchers found the standard deviation figure. In the Stanford-Binet test the standard deviation figure was 16. Applying this to the curve shown in figure 4, we have equal standard deviations above and below the mean. People with an IQ score between 100 and 116 register +1 standard deviation above the mean while those with an IQ score between 84 and 100 register -1 standard deviation below the mean. It will be noted quickly that 68% of the subjects (nearly 7 out of 10) fell either one standard deviation above or below the mean of 100. going up the scale, only 13½ percent of the subjects were in the second standard deviation level with an IQ between 116 and 132. Thus it could be said that a person with an IQ of 132 scored higher than 97.5% of the sample (50% + 34% + 13.5%). The last two levels, approaching and including genius, show only 2½ % in the third standard deviation -132 to 148 and, finally .135% at the fourth level. This example should illustrate how the standard deviation is used to carefully denote the variability from the mean.

Skewed Distribution

Not all distributions are normal, however. Some are asymmetrical. These are called skewed distributions and can be skewed negatively or positively. In both cases, the mean is pulled in the direction of the extreme scores. Thus, for a negatively skewed distribution the mean is always lower or smaller than the median, and for a positively skewed distribution, the mean is always higher or greater than the median. In a negatively skewed distribution, the "tail" of the curve points to the left away from the median and in the positively skewed distribution. The "tail" points toward the right away from the median.

(see figure 11)

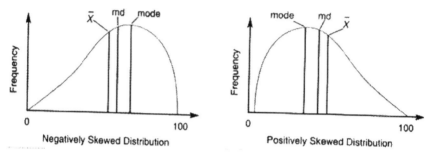

Figure 11

A negatively skewed figure indicates that the majority of the scores were above the mean showing that (in the case of a test) the test way may have been too easy. In the case of a positively skewed picture, the opposite is true. Here the majority of the scores were below the mean indicating that the test could possible have been too hard.

Measure of Relative Position

Measures of relative position are used in norm-referenced scoring. They show where a score is in relation to other scores in the sample that was measured on the same variable. In other words, these measures show how on individual did in relation to others in the same sample.

Percentile Rank

The simplest measure of relative position is the percentile rank. The percentile rank indicates the percentage of scores that fall at or below a given score. Thus, if a given score falls into a percentile rank of 85 or 85%, it means that the score was better than 85% of the other scores. Conversely, a score that falls in the 15% percentile means that the score was only better than 15% of the other scores (and 85% scored higher).

Standard Scores

Standard scores show greater specificity than percentile scores and are usually expressed two ways—the Z score and the T score. The standard scores show how far a raw score (the actual score) is from a reference point (usually the mean) in terms of standard deviation units. Standard scores are appropriate when test data represent interval or ratio scales of measurement (discussed later in this chapter). A big advantage of standard scores is that they allow scores FROM DIFFERENT TESTS to be compared on a common scale.

Z scores

Z scores are the most basis type of standard score and, very simply, show how far the score is from the mean in terms of standard deviation units, the formula for the Z score is as follows:

$Z = \dfrac{X-M}{SD}$ or the score(X) minus the mean (M) over the standard deviation.

For example, a score on two tests might be the same-

MATH SCORE = 70;   VOCABULARY SCORE = 70

Are these scores equivalent? We don't know.

If the mean for both tests is 65, are they equivalent? We still don't know.

Applying the formula will give us the answer.

If the computed standard deviation for the math test is 10 and the standard deviation for the vocabulary test is 5, the formula will yield the following figures:

MAT- $\dfrac{70-65}{10} = \dfrac{5}{10} = \text{½} = .50$

VOCABULARY- $\dfrac{70-65}{5} = \dfrac{5}{5} = 1 = 1.00$

The math score is only one half a standard deviation from the mean while the vocabulary score is one full standard deviation from the mean. Thus, we can see that the vocabulary test score was higher.

T Scores

The only problem with Z scores is that sometimes the numbers are negative (-1 standard deviation from the mean). This is not always an effective (or advisable) way to report scores of students (and their parents) are involved. To compensate for the deficiency, a T score can be used. The formula for this score is:

[Z score times 10 + 50] A Z score of -1. therefore becomes a T score of 40. Thus the new mean becomes 50. Using a normal curve equivalency this can later be transformed into percentiles.

Stanines

Stanine scores can show the relative position of figures in terms of a division of standard deviation units. This allows for more specificity but may not be as easy to read as the T scores. Stanines are standard scores that are divided into nine parts on a scale. The stanine equivalencies are derived by using the formula $2Z + 5$ and rounding the resulting values to the nearest whole. Stanines 2 through 8 each represent ½ SD of the distribution; stanine 1 and 9 include the remainder.

Scales of Measurement

In statistical procedures, there are four types of scales of measurement available to researchers. Each scale has a different level of desirability and each is used for a different purpose. The four scales are presented in hierarchical form.

Nominal Scale

The nominal scale is used when variables differ qualitatively but not quantitatively. Using the root "nom" from the French language meaning "name", the nominal scale could be designated as the "naming scale." On other words, variables are classified by name instead of numbers. Variables on a nominal scale might be listed as groups such as: freshman, sophomores, juniors and seniors. Groups could be classified as education majors, psychology majors or history majors. In other words, all "data" are listed by a qualitative term—by name.

Ordinal Scale

This scale is a very simple scale in that it just contains ranked data. Ordinal scales have unequal units of measurements because the ranking just goes from the lowest to the highest scores but does not tell how the scores differ. A basic use of the ordinal scale would be to rank a group of people from the shortest to the tallest. The ranking does not tell any sort of relationship between the scores (i.e.—"twice as tall," proportions of one height to another"), it just ranks the numbers.

Interval Scale

This scale has equal units of measurements but has no true value of zero. Most of the tests used in educational research use the interval scale. Because of the equal units of measurement, we can assume that the difference between a score of 80 and 90 is essentially the same as the difference between 70 and 80. Because there is no true zero point, however, we could not say that a student who scored a zero on a math test has no knowledge of mathematics. Or, to take the point further, we could not surmise that a student who scored zero on a measure of one's self concept has, in fact, no self concept. Because of this feature, the interval scale has limitations in certain types of research.

Ratio Scale

The ratio scale represents the highest scale of measurement because it does have a true zero point. Weight, time, distance, speed and temperature are all measured on a ratio scale. Thus, it is possible to say that something weighs twice as much as another object, or that a person who is six feet tall is twice as tall as one who measures three feet in height. For this reason, the ratio scale is most desired when making statistical comparisons.

Correlating Ranked Data

In educational research, it is often desirable to see if two variables are related. For instance, is reading comprehension relate to vocabulary acquisition? Is math ability related to one's attitude towards that subject? What is the relationship between musical proficiency and the amount of practice? All of these subjects entail the use of correlational research that begins by correlating ranked data. This correlation can be achieved by informal means or by the use of statistical formulas.

Informal Correlation

Thus far in this chapter, the focus has been on using descriptive statistics to show how a single variable is distributed among a group of people. In making these correlations, the researcher is attempting to see how two variables affect a designated group. For instance, the question of the relationship between reading and vocabulary acquisition might be studied. Students' scores on a science test and a math test could be ranked and plotted as follows.

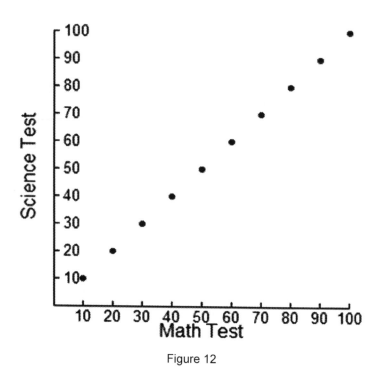

Figure 12

This figure represents a perfect correlation-there is an exact relationship between the two variables. However, a perfect correlation rarely occurs so the plotting is not as easy as this. A more realistic plot of scores might appear as follows:

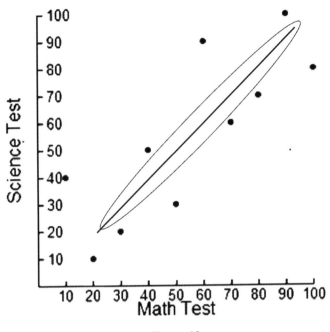

Figure 13

In order to see the correlation in this case, a 45° line must be drawn starting with the intersection of the two lines. Students' scores on each test are then ranked from lowest to highest vertically and horizontally. In the figure above we see that Maria has scored 100 on the science test and 90 on the math test. To see how close this score is to a perfect correlation (indicated by the 45° line), we plot Maria's math score vertically and her science score horizontally until the points meet. At this point we place a dot and we can see that the two scores are close to the line and, thus, are correlated.

Plotting all of the scores in a similar manner, it can be seen that most of the scores fell fairly close to the line. Actually, only three of the ten scores were far from the line. When we connect the dots, the oval figure shows that since both scores were close to the line, there was a strong correlation between the math scores and the science scores. This is not always the case however. Let's look at figure 14 and see if there is a correlation between students' weight and their science scores

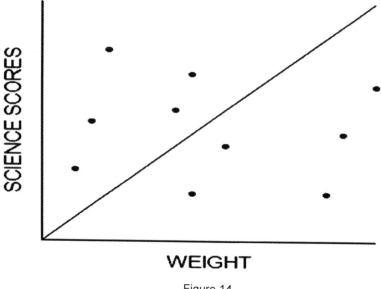

WEIGHT

Figure 14

Here the dots are spaced far apart indication that there is no direct correlation between the two variables.

In other instances there can actually be a negative correlation. This means that instead of the two variables drawing close, they actually draw apart. In other words, as one variable goes up, the other variable goes down. Let's see, for example, the correlation between the temperature of the classroom and the students' level of proficiency on a math test. To plot a negative correlation, we must draw a 45° line the opposite direction from right to left instead of left to right. Here we see that as the temperature of the classroom rises, the level of proficiency goes down.

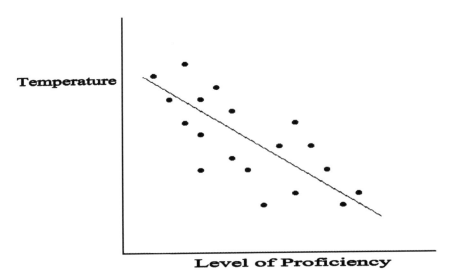

Temperature

Level of Proficiency

Figure 15

A procedure such as this is called "eyeballing" and can be very useful to the classroom teacher. This technique is informal, however, and as such it lacks scientific validity. To gain this scientific validity, it is important to use formal measures of correlation.

Formal Correlation

To obtain a valid measure of correlation, the correlation coefficient must be found. A perfect correlation coefficient must be found. A perfect correlation coefficient is indicated by the figure 1.00 as possible to determine a high degree of comparability.

Although statisticians may disagree on the degree of correlation, it is generally recognized that a correlation above + .65 or -.65 is a high correlation. Between + .35 and + .65 or between -.35 and -.65 is a moderate correlation and figures lower than + .35 and -.35 indicates low correlation or none at all. Depending on the purpose of the study, different degrees of correlation would be acceptable. For a small study not intended for generalizability, a moderate correlation might be sufficient. For a study involving predictability, a larger coefficient might be required.

To interpret a correlation coefficient accurately, it is important to determine how much variability the two variables have in common. If two variables have a correlation coefficient of .80 this does not mean that they are 80% related. Instead, it is necessary to see how much variability in one variable is accounted for by the variability in another variable. This is called the shared variance and is found by squaring the correlation coefficient. Thus variables that have a correlation coefficient of .80 would only have a shared variance of 64%. This means that 36% of the variance between these two variables is still unexplained.

By now, the reader is probably wondering where these figures come from and how they are derived. Since these are formal correlations and, as such, will require degrees of statistical significance, statistical formulas must be used. The two most common formulas must be used. The two most common formulas are the Pearson Product Moment Correlation Coefficient and the Spearman Rho.

The Pearson Product Moment formula is most commonly used in educational research because it is used with ratio or interval data. The Spearman Rho formula is often used with ranked or ordinal data. The Pearson formula is the more precise of the two but the Spearman is easier to compute with a group of subjects less than thirty.

Two other factors come into play when determining the relationship between two variables. These are the linear relationship and the curvilinear relationship. In most correlational problems, the relationship is investigated with the assumption that an increase in one variable corresponds with an increase in another variable(or vice versa if it is a negative relationship). This is called a linear relationship and is illustrated in figure 13.

In a curvilinear relationship, the same is true—up to a point. In other words, an increase in one variable is associated with an increase in another variable until the increase in one variable causes a decrease in the other variable. The best example of this is the curvilinear relationship between age and agility.

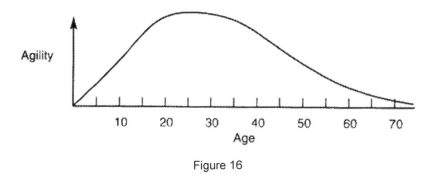

Figure 16

As one grows from infancy to young adulthood, one's agility becomes greater with maturity and muscle development. As this person continues to age, however, a decline in agility is noticed and that variable decreases as age increases, thus the curvilinear effect.

Interestingly, if a relationship becomes curvilinear, a different correlation is necessary for measurement. This coefficient is called the eta coefficient. This is necessary because using a correlational technique for a linear relationship when the relationship is curvilinear will be of no use because it will automatically show no relationship.

Multiple Regression Relationships

Up until now, we have just examined the relationship between two variables. In some instances, the researcher might want to examine several variables to note their effect on one or more dependent variables. This creates a multiple regression equation. Since correlational research is often used for prediction purposes, we could do a study to determine if there is a relationship between a student's score on the SAT and his or her grade point average in later years in college. These two variables have been shown to correlate and this is why SAT scores are used for college entrance exams.

Many college admission offices, however, choose to include other factors as well for admission requirements. Some of these factors are: high school grades, letters of recommendations, written essays and personal interviews. When these other points are factored into the correlation equation we have a multiple regression equation. (also called a multiple prediction equation).

Summary

This chapter presented an overview of descriptive research from the measures of central tendency, the measures of variability to the correlation of ranked data. It was shown that descriptive statistics are used to show how a particular characteristic is distributed among a group. Information was also shown to illustrate how factors are related through correlations. In the next chapter, we will go a step further and present inferential statistics.

Chapter 6

Understanding Inferential Statistics

The previous chapter was devoted to the study of descriptive statistics—the process of describing quantitatively how variables are distributed among a group of subjects. In other words, this brand of statistics—simplistically speaking—analyzes what currently exists. Inferential statistics, however, takes the analysis a bit further and shows what might be or what could be. Using the root word "infer", inferential statistics are used to make inferences about current data. This brand of statistics allows the researcher to generalize the findings of a study to another similar population.

Two important considerations aligned with inferential statistics are "time" and "replication". For example, suppose a study was conducted that offered statistical proof that a certain method of teaching reading produced superior reading results in a group of second grade students. Before this method was put to use on a full-scale basis, a prudent administrator might question the results and ask the researcher "Can you do this study again and gain the same results?" If the second study produced the same results, another very cautious administrator might say, "I'd like to see the same results three times in a row." At this point, an exasperated researcher might exclaim, "How many times do I have to replicate this study in order to prove its effectiveness?"

By using inferential statistics properly, however, no replication is necessary. Inferential statistics will show the mathematical PROBABILITY that the results will be the same if the population and the procedures are identical. Further, if the logistics and the population are highly similar, inferential statistics can show the mathematical chances that the results could be produced in another population. Thus, the application of inferential statistics can save the researcher time and effort of replication while proving the validity and reliability of the results. If done correctly, the use of these statistics allows a researcher to carry out a study only once and generalize the findings to an entire population.

Statistical Significance

In using inferential statistics, the first thing the researcher should do is establish a probability zone or level. This is the zone that allows for the probability of error and is denoted as the alpha level. Most researchers will operate with an alpha level of 95%. This is to say that, statistically speaking—there is a 95% chance that the results of a study are accurate and can be generalized without replication. Therefore, the probability of error is only 5%.

Another way of explaining this point is to use the term "statistical significance." In most research studies, an acceptable degree of statistical significance is the .05 level. This means that if the study were replicated 100 times there would be only a .05 chance (or five in one hundred) that the results would differ. For most research projects, a 95% success rate is acceptable. Anything below this level, however, could NOT be deemed STATISTICALLY SIGNIFICANT. In some research projects, the level of significance is set at the .01 level. This means that only 1% chance of failure is acceptable. When these levels of statistical significance are pre-determined and then proved statistically, the project can be deemed a success and the results can be generalized to a demographically similar population without question.

Degrees of Freedom

When carrying out research using samples of a population, it is necessary to estimate the variability of the scores within the population. Statistically, variability found within samples underestimates the actual variability within a population. This is due to the fact that extreme scores that appear in the population are less likely to appear in the sample, therefore, the larger the underestimate.

To compensate for this underestimation, researchers reduce the sample size by one. The term used to indicate that the sample size has been reduced by one is Degrees of Freedom (df). Author Thomas K. Crowl explained the concept of Degrees of Freedom as follows:

> "One calculates the mean of a sample to obtain an estimate of the mean of the population from which the sample has been drawn. Once the mean is calculated, the number of scores that may vary and still yield the same mean is one less than the number of scores." (Crowl 1996)

The Confidence Interval and the Standard Error of the Mean

The confidence interval is a range of numbers within which the true mean of the population exists. There are two ways to determine this confidence interval. One is to add the means of the samples and thus calculate the true mean. This method, of course, could be cumbersome and might require quite a bit of time.

The second method is to <u>infer </u>what the confidence level might be by using the standard error of the mean. The word "error" indicates an "error of estimate"(discussed previously). The standard error of the mean, therefore, tells how much the sample means would differ if other samples from the same population were used. The standard error of the mean can be estimated from the standard deviation of a single sample by using the formula:

$$SEx = \frac{SD}{\sqrt{N-1}}$$

Where:

SEx = the standard error of the mean

SD = the standard deviation of the sample
N = the sample size
A sample would appear as follows:
(x) Mean = 75
    SD = 16
    N = 65

$$SEx = \frac{16}{65-1} = \frac{16}{\sqrt{64}} = \frac{16}{8} = 2$$

SEx = 2

The confidence interval then is ± 2 or 73-77.

The Null Hypothesis and Tests of Significance

Most research studies will begin by stating an hypothesis or hypotheses or else by stating research questions. In either case, the results are proved (or disproved) by showing levels of statistical significance.

When using the hypothesis method, there are three types of hypotheses. These are the directional hypothesis, the non-directional hypothesis and the null hypothesis. In an experiment comparing one reading method to another reading method for effectiveness in learning, a directional hypothesis would state that Method A would prove to be more effective than Method B by applying statistics of scores that show levels of significance of .05 or better.

A non-directional hypothesis is less definitive. This hypothesis would predict that there would be a statistically significant difference in the scores from the two methods of teaching reading but it would not predict which method would prevail. A null hypothesis, on the other hand, would predict that there would be no difference statistically in the scores from both methods.

When using the directional or the non-directional hypotheses, the results are usually quite evident as shown by the level of statistical significance. When using the null hypothesis, two types of errors can occur in decision making. A TYPE 1 Error occurs when the researcher rejects the null hypothesis (there is no difference) when the results show that it is true (there is a difference). The TYPE 2 Error occurs when the opposite happens. A researcher accepts the null hypothesis (there is no difference) when the results say it is false (there is a difference).

To illustrate this point, there are four possibilities when accepting or rejecting the null hypothesis:

1- The null hypothesis is true (there is no difference) and the researcher accepts this hypothesis based on the statistical significance.

2- The null hypothesis is false (there is a difference) and the researcher rejects the null hypothesis based on the statistical significance.

3- The null hypothesis is true (there is no difference) but the researcher rejects the null hypotheses and says it is false—A TYPE 1 ERROR.

4- The null hypothesis is false (there is a difference) but the researcher accepts the null hypotheses and says it is true—A TYPE 2 Error.

Two Tailed and One Tailed Tests

These types of hypotheses can be graphed by the use of one-tailed or two tailed tests of significance. The "tails" in this case represent the extreme ends of the bell-shaped curve of a normal distribution. A one-tailed test would be used with a directional hypothesis, i.e. there will be a difference shown in the results of a study and it will be statistically significant in one direction. The two-tailed test can be used with a non-directional hypothesis to show that there will be a difference in the results of the study but it will be statistically significant either negatively or positively. This point is illustrated by the following figure.

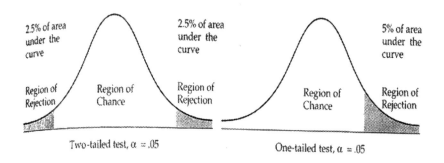

Two-tailed test, $\alpha = .05$ One-tailed test, $\alpha = .05$

Figure 1

It is shown here that if the level of significance is set at the .05 level, the one-tailed test indicates the margin of error in one direction (in this case at the top of the curve). The two-tailed test, on the other hand, splits the margin of error to 2.5% and allows for error to be either at the top or the bottom of the curve. Both the one-tailed and the two-tailed test can be used with a null hypothesis.

Tests of Significance

Different tests of significance are used for different types of data. The first decision the researcher must make is whether to use a parametric or a non-parametric test. Three conditions must be met in order to use a parametric test. These conditions are: (a) the variable measured must be in the form of a normal distribution (or the form of the distribution is known), (b) the data represent an interval or ratio scale of measurement, (c) the selection of the subjects is independent—that is, the selection of one subject does not affect the selection of other subjects.

The criteria for a non-parametric test are exactly opposite—the distribution is not known, the data are in normal or ordinal form and the selection of subjects is not independent. Since most measures in education are based on data ranked on an interval or ratio scale, the parametric type of test is most frequently used.

The t Test

The t test is a parametric test used to determine if TWO means are significantly different at a selected probability level. For example, suppose a researcher has a research question (or a hypothesis) that administrators views on the subject of inclusion of children with special needs in a regular classroom were significantly different from those classroom teachers. A survey could be given to both groups of subjects (the administrators and the teachers). Means would be drawn from the data supplied by both groups. The t test would then be used to determine the level of statistical significance. If the .05 level of significance came out higher than .05 (say, .07 or .08), it could be proved that administrators have a significantly DIFFERENT view of inclusion than classroom teachers. In a statistical study such as this, the level of statistical significance is indicated by p, which represents the probability that the findings of the study are incorrect. Therefore, a p< .05 (probability less than .05) means than there are 95 chances in 100 that the findings based on the samples would be the same if different population were used.

The t Test for Independent and Non-Independent Samples

The t test for independent samples is a parametric test of significance used to determine whether, at a selected probability level, a significant difference exists between the means of the two independent samples (Gay, Mills and Airasian—2006). In this instance, independent samples mean two randomly formed groups without any type of matching.

In like manner, the t test for non-independent samples is used to compare groups that are formed by some type of matching (such as for a pre-test and a post-test) or where the members of the groups are systematically related (such as comparing a group's scores or achievement levels from one year to the next). Both of these types of tests require different formulas in order to arrive at a valid conclusion.

The Analysis of Variance (ANOVA)

While the t test was used to compare the differences in two means, the analysis of variance (ANOVA) is used to compare the differences in more than two means. Using the previous example, a researcher might want to know the differences in opinion about inclusion from three groups—administrators, secondary teachers and elementary teachers. If desired, a further breakdown could be made for males and females.

A relevant question here might be "Why not just use continuous t tests?" Although this could be done, the chance of error is greater with continuous calculations of t tests. It is simpler and more efficient, therefore, to use just one test—the analysis of variance.

This type of ANOVA is called a one-way ANOVA because there is only one variable in question by the various groups—the variable of opinions about inclusion of special education students in the regular classroom. The concept underlying ANOVA is that the total variation or variance, of scores can be divided into two sources—variance between groups and variance within groups. (Gay, Mills, and Airasian—2006)

In order to account for these variances, an F ratio must be formed with group differences as the numerator (variance between groups) and variance within groups (error variance) as the denominator. The greater the difference in the fraction, the larger the F ratio will be. From here, the researcher must consult an F table to determine if the ratio is significant at the place corresponding to the selected probability level and the appropriate degrees of freedom.

Higher Order ANOVAS

In the previous paragraphs, the one-way ANOVA was shown—the case where there is only one variable. On some occasions, however, more than one variable is studied; this entails a higher order ANOVA—possibly a two-way or three—way ANOVA. This study is illustrated as follows:

One-Way ANOVA—3 Means

Variable	Administrators	Secondary Teachers	Elementary Teachers
Opinion of inclusion			
	M1	M2	M3

Two-Way ANOVA—6 Means

Variable	Administrators	Secondary Teachers	Elementary Teachers
Opinions of inclusion; males and females			

MALE	M1	M2	M3
FEMALE	M4	M5	M6

Three-Way ANOVA—12 Means

Variables		Administrators		Secondary Teachers		Elementary Teachers	
		Male	Female	Male	Female	Male	Female
Opinion of inclusion; males and females; large school and small school	LARGE SCHOOL	M1	M2	M3	M4	M5	M6
	SMALL SCHOOL	M7	M8	M9	M10	M11	M12

Multivariate Analysis (MANOVA)

The multivariate Analysis (MANOVA) is also called a multiple regression analysis. It is used when two or more groups are studied with a multitude of variables. For example, suppose a researcher wanted to examine the question of why one school had a higher dropout rate than another school. In order to do this study correctly, a variety of groups should be studied in comparison with a number of factors. The arrangement would be as follows:

Dependent Variable = Dropout Rate

Factors
-Socio-economic Level
-Education of parents
-Cultural Values
-Parental Expectations

Groups
-Divided by age
-Males
-Females
-Race
-Culture

As one can imagine, a study such as this would have a high degree of difficulty and would take a substantial amount of time to complete.

Analysis of Covariance—(ANCOVA)

An excellent and compact definition of the analysis of covariance is provided by author Thomas Crowl:

> "the analysis of covariance is a way of taking pretest scores that are different and adjusting them statistically so that they can be treated as being identical" (Crowl, 1996)

A common use of this tool is in causal-comparative studies in which data is gathered after the fact. For example, when making a comparison of the buying power of the dollar in 1929 and the present day, various statistics could be gathered from the past and adjustments made to make past and present data identical. This would entail weighting several factors until accurate comparisons could be made through the ANCOVA formula.

Chi Square (x^2)

Up to this point, all of the formulas for inferential statistics have dealt with interval or ratio data. The chi square formula is different because it deals with nominal data. The chi square test is a non-parametric test that is used when the data are in the form of frequency counts, percentages and proportions that can be converted to actual numbers. The formula for calculating chi square is as follows:

Chi square (x^2) = $\Sigma \dfrac{(O\text{-}E)\,2}{E}$

Where O = observed number of cases in a category (actual)

E = expected number of cases in a category (depending on the hypothesis or research question)

Σ = Sum

The chi square can best be illustrated by an example from Thomas Crowl in <u>Fundamentals of Educational Research.</u>

Research Problem

Is there a relationship between a student's gender and the type of disability? Further, are there proportionally more girls or boys among learning disabled (LD), emotionally disturbed (ED) and physically disabled (PD) students?

<u>Step 1</u>—Sample 100 disabled students

<u>Step 2</u>—Find the actual numbers in each category

    a. 26 girls are either LD, ED, or PD (26%)

    b. 74 boys are either LD, ED, or PD (74%)

<u>Step 3</u>—Show the Actual Distribution

Actual Distribution

	LD	ED	PD	Total	%
Girls	12	5	9	26	26%
Boys	20	37	17	74	74%
Total	32	42	26	100	100%

<u>Step 4</u>—Returning to the research question, we might expect an equal distribution of boys and girls with each disability.

For example—there are 32 LD students—to be consistent we might expect 26% to be girls and 74% to be boys. The Expected Distribution in this category, therefore, would be:

26% of 32 = 8.32 students

74% of 32 = 23.68 students

Returning to the actual distribution, however, reveals that this is not the case. The actual distribution shows that-

	LD		Total		
Girls	12	of	26	=	37.4%
Boys	20	of	74	=	66.6%

There is actually a higher percentage of girls in the LD category than was expected and a lower percentage of boys that was expected.

Step 5—We must now find the discrepancy in the distribution.

Discrepancy Analysis

LD

Girls   12.00 students (Actual)

Girls   8.32 students (Expected)

Girls   3.68 students (Discrepancy)

LD

Boys   20.00 students (Actual)

Boys   23.68 students (Expected)

Boys   -3.68 students (Discrepancy)

Step 6- Apply the formula

$$x^2 = \Sigma \frac{(O-E)^2}{E}$$

$$x^2 = 7.54$$

Step 7—Determine the significance

Step 7 is accomplished by referring to a chi square table of statistics. This shows that a figure of 7.54 with 2 df has a statistical significance of $p<.05$.

<u>Step 8</u>—Return to research questions.

Our data shows, therefore, that the answer to the first part of the research question is "yes"—there is a statistically significant relationship between gender and the type of disability. The second part of the research question is also true—the proportions among the category LD are not equal. Note: to fully complete the research questions, these calculations must be completed for each category listed.

<u>Summary</u>

In this chapter, the difference between descriptive statistics and inferential statistics was shown. It was described how inferential statistics can save both time and replication effort by applying statistical significance which permits generalizations to be made to similar samples from the same population or like populations.

Tests of statistical significance were presented to include the t tests, one-way ANOVA, higher order ANOVAS, the MANOVA, ANCOVA, and chi square. In the next chapter, steps in preparing a master's thesis or a doctoral dissertation will be shown.

Chapter 7

How Theses and Dissertations are Written

Although there are different formats for writing theses and dissertations—some are organized in five, six or seven chapters—the content of those chapters usually contains the same fixtures. The format presented in this chapter is the five chapter format which consists of the Introduction, the Literature Review, the Explanation of Methodology, the Presentation of Results, the Summary and Implications for Future Research.

Writing for Research Papers

Writing for research papers is unlike any other type of writing in that it is very formal and impersonal. This is done on purpose because the researcher must give the impression of being detached and objective. In most research writing the use of personal pronouns such as "I" or "We" is forbidden. In addition, all forms of colloquial expressions or slang expressions are omitted. Further, the writer is not permitted to enter any personal opinions and is discouraged from using any editorial-type comments or statements.

In proper research writing, all statements must be substantiated by references to the original source or by quotations from that source. Thus, the writer is allowed very little room for personal comments or freedom for creativity of expression. This is done on purpose because the paper, itself, is a presentation of RESEARCH that is intended to enlighten the reader or to answer research questions or hypotheses.

Because of the unique nature of research writing, it is difficult for the writer to adapt to this style initially. In fact, research writing is probably the exact OPPOSITE of any style of writing previously done by the writer. Think of it—no self expression, no personal comments, no editorializing—in short, no drama or excitement that is usually present in other forms of writing. To get a clear picture of this style of writing, it may be wise to obtain a completed thesis or dissertation and study the actual format.

Chapter 1—The Introduction

Chapter one sets the stage for the rest of the paper and, because of this, it is of top importance. This chapter answers the questions—"What?" "Where?" "Why?" and "Who?" Here the writer explains what he or she plans to do. This is spelled out explicitly and research questions or hypotheses are included. The significance of the study is presented to show the reader why the project is important. The "Where" and "Who" denote the demographics and explain the characteristics of the population studied.

Although chapter one is, in itself, an introductory chapter, it is also begun with an introduction. This introduction—usually just a page or two—tells the national scope of the issues covered in the study. Once again, all references are cited and the text is free from the author's opinions or ideas. Once the national arena has been covered, the author brings the issue down to the local level. Here the author relates why the study is important locally. This is the statement of purpose and this can be covered by a half page to one page. Following the presentation of the purpose of the study, the writer covers the "who" and "where" questions by showing the demographic characteristics of the community and the school or schools in question.

Once the purpose of the study has been ascertained, the writer gives a brief explanation of what he or she plans to research. This explanation does not have to be made in great detail (that will come later) but it should be lengthy enough so that the reader can put the study in proper context. Specific references are then made in the form of research questions of hypotheses.

These two features are not the same and usually one or the other is used in a study. Research questions are the key questions that the research study seeks to answer. Hypothesis, on the other hand, are presented in the form of "educated guesses" of what the researcher expects to find. At any rate, these two features are of paramount importance, they are the essence of the study and, as such, great care must be taken in their selection and writing.

These questions or hypotheses should be developed in conjunction with the researcher's major advisor. In many cases they are written and re-written many times over a period of weeks before the advisor gives approval. This procedure may be considered the most important feature of the entire study because faulty research resulting in faulty conclusions. Some exemplary research questions and hypotheses are presented next.

Non-Directional Hypothesis

There will be a significant difference in Middle School Practices between high-reading achievement and low-reading achievement middle schools.

Directional Hypothesis

There will be a positive statistical correlation between the community college funding in this state and the number of students transferring to the state university,

Null Hypothesis

There will be no significant difference in Middle School Practices associated with transition programs in high-mathematics achievement and low-mathematics achievement middle schools.

Research Questions

1-What kinds of literacy-enriched activities help prepare preschool children for formal schooling and reading readiness?

2-Is there a significant difference in reading growth scores from the supplemental Four Block reading instruction and the Reading Mastery I reading program?

Limitations and Delimitations

Two distinct cautions that should concern the researcher are the limitations and delimitations of the study. The limitations explain the restrictions of the study and the delimitations cover the scope or boundaries of the project. For example, the study may be restricted to students in the regular classroom and will not encompass students with special needs or students whose first language is not English. In reviewing the scope or boundary of the study, the researcher could explain that is only includes a population from one school or possibly one specific area of the school district or region.

A final section of the first chapter is the definition of terms used in the study. It is important to note that this section includes any abbreviations or acronyms used, any "working definitions" ("for the purpose of this study, the term "administrator" will include only the school principal or any assistant principals") and only those definitions that are unique to the study. It is not only unnecessary but superfluous to include definitions such as "school", "student" or "grade level" unless it carries a different meaning in the exact setting that is being used.

Lastly, the writer should provide a brief overview of the rest of the project by explaining what is to be contained in the following chapters. As in any well-written chapter, a short summary of chapter one should be included.

Chapter 2—the Review of the Literature

By far, the lengthiest chapter of the thesis or dissertation is the review of the literature. Depending on the type of study and the topic researched, this chapter could be from 30-70 pages.

The purpose of the literature review is to give the researcher the opportunity to show that he or she has examined a thorough representation of the current and relevant literature surrounding the topic. In this instance the words "current" and "relevant" are of paramount importance. Unless the literature has an historical significance, all references should be as current as possible. Any references that are ten years old or more could be considered to be out of date. Care must also be taken to ensure that the literature presented should be directly germane to the topic under study.

The literature review should be a skillfully blended narrative of similar research that has been conducted on the selected topic by published authors. Once again, there is no need to present opinions, personal commentary or editorial references in this section. The object here is for the writer to demonstrate to the reader that he or she has properly examined what has been done before in regard to the topic and to assure the reader that the study will add to the meaningful research on that subject.

The previous research presented should be taken from established research journals of the refereed nature, this is to say that no popular-type journal should be used as well as digests or reprinted summations. The use of the word "narrative" is emphasized because the literature review is more than an annotated bibliography of a list of research projects. As with most good writing, transitions should be used between points and information should be blended in a readable form. It is advisable, therefore, to use sub-headings to separate the various sections.

A good literature review might begin with a brief reiteration of the topic and the purpose of the research. In some cases, it might be appropriate to present a brief history of the subject. For example, if one's topic is about the subject of mainstreaming, in order to put the current topic in historical perspective. In this case, it would be appropriate to use references that are older than ten years. From the past, the writer could work to the present showing the progression of the subject through the years. Next would come the national, state, or even local literature that supports the topic.

Some writers like to use the research questions or the hypotheses as a structure for the literature review. This allows for clarity of understanding on the part of the reader. Care must be taken, however, to display an unbiased review of the literature. Using the subject of mainstreaming, once again, the writer should show literature on BOTH SIDES of the question when possible. Therefore, it is important to present some "negative" literature in order to demonstrate an UNBIASED VIEW.

Finally, the writer should identify the direction that the study will take and should show how the results will add to the existing literature in the field. Once again, to use proper form, the chapter should include a brief summary and provide a transition to the next chapter. Before beginning to write the chapter, it would be wise for the researcher to examine completed theses or dissertations for guidance.

Chapter 3—The Methodology

In chapter one, the questions "What?", "Why?", "Where? and "Who" were addressed. Chapter three defines the "How?" for the reader. Precisely how will the study be conducted? This must be answered fully to the satisfaction of the reader. As with the other chapters, chapter three is begun with a brief introduction that provides a transition from the previous chapter. Following this the purpose of the project is restated and the research questions or hypotheses repeated.

Next, the writer explains the type of study that will be used. These types include the quantitative, the qualitative or the mixed method approached. Whatever approach is chosen, it must be fully explained to the reader. Once again, citations from research textbooks should be used to explain the approach.

Once this has been explained, the exact method to be employed should be presented. One of six common methods of research are usually used. These methods are: descriptive, correlational, ex-post facto, experimental, quasi-experimental or case study. In like manner, the methodology chosen must be fully explained to the reader using appropriate citations and references. The reason for these explanations is to assure the reader that the researcher is completely knowledgeable about the type of research and the methodology employed.

After the methodology has been covered, the researcher describes how the data will be collected. Common methods of collecting data include using a survey, an interview, a questionnaire or observational techniques. Any method used to collect data should be explained in detail. For instance, if a survey or a questionnaire is selected, the researcher should explain if it is a professionally prepared instrument or a personally constructed device. If it is a professionally constructed instrument, the researcher needs to explain where and how it was validated and if permission was obtained from the author before using it.

If the device was personally constructed by the researcher, he or she should explain when and how it was field tested and what revisions were made. These same criteria apply to the use of interview questions. In addition, the researcher needs to explain how the data were recorded, by hand on the spot, by memory or by video or tape. In the case of an observation, the criteria are a bit different. Here, a rubric should be employed to denote what behaviors are being observed. In order to guard against bias in observing, it is necessary (whenever possible) to employ the technique of triangulation.

Triangulation is a technique in which three observers are used at the same time. Results are then compared and extreme scores are eliminated. This technique can prove to be highly efficient in compensating for possible observer bias. A difficulty with the use of triangulation, however, is that the researcher must use trained observers for the task and if no trained observers are available, the researcher must do all the preliminary training of the assistants.

Following the explanation of the data collection procedures, the writer describes how the data will be analyzed and applied to the hypotheses or research questions. This explanation should carefully delineate the type of statistics employed. Depending upon the method of research and the hypotheses or research questions, different statistics might be used. A researcher might wish to present only the mean, median and standard deviation to illustrate the measures of central tendency.

At other times, statistical procedures such as a t test, analysis of variance or analysis of covariance would be utilized. In correlational studies, the Pearson Product Moment or the Spearman Rho formulas are applied.

Whatever statistics are used, however, it is the writer's duty to describe the procedure and to explain why that particular method was appropriate. When all of this information is provided, the chapter on Methodology is complete. In actuality, the three chapters just mentioned—the Introduction, the Literature Review and the explanation of the Methodology—constitute the research proposal. These three chapters are written in the future tense because they propose what will be done. Once the proposal is accepted by the research committee, permission is granted to conduct the research according to the terms presented.

Chapter 4—Analysis of Results

This chapter is written at the conclusion of the study and now the tense shifts from the future tense to the past tense. At this time, the data collection procedures are reviewed and verified and the research questions or hypothesis are re-introduced. The researcher then presents the findings and applies those findings to answer the research questions and prove or disprove the hypothesis. This proof may be presented in the form of tables, charts or graphs and should be supplemented by a strong narrative. Extreme care should be taken to avoid the appearance of bias or prejudice. Sufficient detail must be provided to convince the reader that the problems posed by the questions or hypothesis have been solved. While the writer's voice is heard a little more in this chapter, care must be taken to let the data "speak for itself".

Chapter 5—Summary of Findings and Implications For Future Research

Here, at long last, the voice of the writer emerges. It is now permissible for the researcher to interject his or her opinions, conclusions or analysis (while still using the impersonal tense). Difficulties encountered in the research may be presented and limitations of delimitations re-introduced.

Because no research is considered to be complete, implications and directions for future study are customarily included. With a concise summary of the chapter, the writing of the thesis or dissertation is concluded and the writer is free to turn his or her attention to the construction of the reference and appendices sections.

Summary

In this chapter the method of writing research papers has been presented. It was emphasized that the impersonal voice should be used with no personal comments or editorializing. With the exception of the final two chapters, the future tense is always utilized. The tense is switched to the past in chapter 4 and, finally, the researcher's voice is heard in the discussion of chapter five.

Chapter 8

A Sample Study Employing Mixed Methods

Author's Note: This chapter was taken from my dissertation for the faculty of the University of Pennsylvania. The dissertation was entitled, "New York City School Principals' Perception of their Role as School Leaders". Sumita Kaufhold.

The mixed-methods approach originally emerged from the field of psychology. This concept was used to triangulate the data collected from several sources and is frequently used in social and behavioral research. Intramethod mixing, also known as data triangulation, in the mixed-methods approach combines qualitative and quantitative approaches in a single study in order to complement the strengths and compensate the weakness of each approach (Tashakkori & Teddlie, 2002). Using the mixed-methods approach allowed the researcher to combine both the quantitative (survey) and qualitative (interviews and field observations) data in order to better understand the research question, which is to understand how New York City principals understand their role within the context of their work setting. Since this study focused on principals' perception of their role as school leaders, a mixed-method design approach appeared to be most applicable.

Goal and Purpose of the Study

The purpose of the study was to investigate from different data instruments how New York City principals understand their role. New York City principals are considered by their school system to be key levers of change in New York City public schools' school-improvement reform movement. New York City public schools have found it difficult to consistently meet the annual accountability measures set by the state or federal government regarding student performance. In addressing this student performance gap, New York City public schools embarked on a full-scale school reform initiative, Children First. This study's goal was to find out how New York City public school principals understand their roles as school teachers within the context of their school-reform initiative.

Methods of Data Collection

The data collection included interviews, a focus group, field observations, and surveys. Thirty-eight principals were invited to participate in an online survey, and 26 completed the survey. These were 10 individual interviews with principals and one focus group consisting of five principals, as well as five elementary school field observational visits. The interviews and focus group were taped. The online survey comprised the quantitative part in the study, whereas the interviews, focus group, and field observations encompassed the qualitative part.

Maxwell (2005) and Rubin and Rubin (2005) have stressed that during the interviews, the participant and researchers need to establish a comfortable rapport while the researcher is asking questions. The relationship between researcher and participants can be complex, as the interview process allowed for a closer examination of beliefs, values, and overall culture that guides the behaviors of principals. The responsive interviewing model was employed, since it encourages the interpretation of the interviewees' experience and understanding of their world. This model of interviewing was flexible and adaptive, and allowed for a more open exchange between the interviewer and interviewee. "In responsive interviewing, as in all naturalist research, the researcher is the instrument, the tool of discovery". (Rubin & Rubin, 2005).

The reason for selecting this model was that the researcher was an insider, which makes this model a natural fit for interviewing known and unknown participants with a shared experience of being a part of New York City Public Schools. The limitations of interviews are that they are time-consuming and can be an intensive process. Interview transcription and subsequent analysis also can be a very lengthy and tedious process.

Focus Group

The purpose of conducting the focus group was to have another forum to gather information and opinion of participants. It allowed the researcher to elicit from participants a range of feelings and thoughts around a discussion topic. It also provided the researcher an opportunity to listen, and to see how people think and feel about a topic in a comfortable and nonstressful environment. "The intent of the focus group was to promote self-disclosure among participants. We want to know what people really think and feel" (Krueger & Casey, 2009). This group discussion permitted the researcher to identify trends and patterns, and gain further insight on the subject matter being investigated; within this forum, organizational issues and concerns might emerge. The focus group consisted of five principals and was voluntary. The reason for selecting five people is because when the purpose of the study is to understand an issue, or if the topic is complex, it is recommended that fewer people be invited to participate in the focus group. When there are fewer people, then there are usually more questions, which may allow for a more in-depth discussion about a topic.

The limitations of the focus group are that one person's response can influence another person's response to a given question. Another factor that might arise in a focus group is that a few people might dominate the conversation and prevent broad participation in the discussion. Time is also a limitation; not having enough time to really delve deeply into a topic, considering the participants' busy schedules, is a legitimate concern. Being unable to capture body language in a discussion or on a tape recorder also can be a limitation.

To address some of the limitations of focus groups, the pause and probe technique was used, which requests that participants elaborate and/or provide additional information. The researcher started a new question with a participant who has conversed less, in order to offset one person dominating the responses. Since body language is hard to capture on tape, the researcher may make symbols or jot down the body language of participants to recall later (Krueger and Casey, 2009).

Field Observations

The field observation consisted of five school visits to elementary schools for part of the day. The researcher visited the elementary schools upon the principals' invitation, elementary schools were chosen because of the researcher's access to these schools. Visiting five schools allowed for triangulation of the data collected from the interviews, focus group, and online survey; these five would be a subset of those who had interviewed and taken the online survey. These five observations served as a representative sample of what occurs in a day in the life of a principal. The researcher observed the activities in which the principal engaged in for half of the day in order to see what processes the principals use to make daily decisions and enact their role. Following the field observation, there was a discussion with the principal in which the researcher asked clarifying questions of what was observed, as well as conducted an interview.

The procedure used in the field observations was based on naturalistic observation, which is a nonexperimental method involving systematic observation of participations in their natural setting (Spata, 2003). The strength of using naturalistic observation was that it permitted the researcher to observe the participants in their natural setting, without any external constraints. The limitation in using naturalistic observation is that, because there are no variables being manipulated in the study, causality cannot be established.

By keeping field notes and interviewing the principal after the field observation was completed, broad questions were developed regarding the conceptual framework:

- What actions or observable behaviors does the principal engage in that fits into the framework of analysis of the role of principal as an accountability manager, organizational manager, and instructional and sociopolitical leader?
- What occurs today as representative of a day in the life of the principals?
- What activity does the principal select to engage in today and why?
- How does he/she prioritize responsibilities in order to address the issues he faced today?
- What does the school principal value; what matters to him/her?
- To what extent does this principal view his/her own role?
- What do they consider as constraints/challenges and strengths in enacting the role as principal?

Online Survey

The quantitative part of the study was done by a survey of 30 principals. These principals were from an intact group under the researcher's direction, the survey consisted of five open-ended questions and 31 closed questions.

Miles and Huberman (1994) recommended software assistance in the research process. They found in a survey that three-fourths of researchers were using computer software for entering data, coding, search and retrieval, making displays, or building concepts. SPSS software was used in coding; such a definitive system of collecting, recording, and analyzing data certainly aided the researcher. An online service, Survey Monkey, was used to administer the survey, making it more accessible to the principals. A school principal might want to participate in this study but not have time for a 30 minute interview; having the option to complete the survey online gave principals the opportunity to complete the survey at a time that was convenient for them, based on the flexibility of their schedule. An additional benefit of the computerized survey was that if principals are unable to complete the survey all at once, their responses were saved, and they could complete the remainder at their convenience.

Protocol Procedures

As with most scientific studies there are various systems of protocol that must be followed in order to ensure the validity of the data received. In reality, this is a code that also prescribes strict adherence to correct etiquette and rules of procedure.

Interview Protocol

Prior to starting the interview, the researcher explained to the principal the purpose of the study and briefly informed them why the researcher was engaged in the study and permission to tape the interview was requested. They were assured that the interview was confidential and that they would remain anonymous. Their responses would be used for the purposes of this study only. Participants had the option of removing themselves from the study at any point of the data collection.

Focus Group Protocol

The focus group's purpose was to ascertain the thoughts, feelings, beliefs, and perceptions of principals regarding their role. Unlike the other data sources, the focus group allowed participants to be spontaneous and to choose whether or not to respond to the comments of other participants during the interview process. It was another direct observation tool, since the researcher was able to record the body language of the participants while they responded to or listened to a given response. Participants were informed of the purpose of the study, and permission to tape the interview was requested. They were assured that their participation in the focus group and their responses were confidential and would remain anonymous. Their responses would only be used as data for this study.

Field Observation Protocol

The school visits for the field observations were voluntary and had the principals' consent. The researcher conducted five elementary school observations of principals, shadowing them for part of the day. The purpose of the field observations as well as the study was explained to the principals. Assurance was given to the principals that the information gathered would be confidential and used only for the purposes of this study.

It was agreed that the principals who participated in the observations would remain confidential. These principals were also interviewed following the visit. After the interview there was a debriefing session between the researcher and the principal where the researcher asked clarifying questions on the observation that just occurred as well as his/ her perception of the principal's role.

Survey Protocol

Participation in the survey was voluntary, and participants could withdraw any time they wished, the participants received a cover letter introducing the study and stating its purpose. The researcher made herself available via email and telephone to answer any questions the participants might have had.

Data Analysis

Spradley (1979) defines "analysis of any kind involves a way of thinking. It refers to the systematic examination of something to determine its parts, the relationship among parts and their relationship to the whole" (Tashakkori & Teddlie, 2010). This broad definition of analysis is applied to the data analysis description of Glesne (2006), who suggests that data analysis is a process involving "organizing what you have seen, heard, and read so that you can make sense of what you have learned. Working with the data, you describe, create explanations, pose hypotheses, develop theories, and link your story to other stories. To do so, you must categorize, synthesize, search for patterns, and interpret the data you have collected" (p. 147). Analysis was a continuous and sequential process (Krueger & Casey, 2009), during which the researcher identified themes in order to ascertain the most important points from each data source, to find out what was surprising or unexpected, and to collect quotes that were helpful in describing the story or elaborating a specific point. Throughout the analysis, the researcher identified emerging patterns. Marshall and Rossman (2006) recommended placing these recurring patterns onto a visual data display such as a matrix. They also shared Patton's (2002) view of data analysis, describing the processes of inductive analysis as "discovering patterns, themes, and categories" (p. 159). Saldana (2009) cites Rossman & Rallis's work where they explain the difference between codes and themes, which is to "think of a category as a *word or phrase* describing some segment of your data that is *explicit,* whereas a theme is a *phrase or sentence* describing more *subtle and tacit processes"* (p. 13).

Computerized software, namely SPSS, was used to code the qualitative data. The descriptive notes from the interviews were transcribed through a transcription service. Creswell (2009) recommended an approach to data analysis whereby the researcher tries to holistically get a sense of the whole thing by reading all the transcriptions carefully, jotting notes as ideas come to mind, making notes on your thoughts in the margins as you read, generating a list of topics that emerge, and categorizing the topics. He suggested coding each topic in order to organize a preliminary scheme, which in my case consisted of the perceptions of the principals and also analyzing four roles as conceptualized in the framework. He also recommended assembling the data by categories and doing a preliminary analysis. There were several sorting of the data through various techniques such as thematic clustering, language analysis in order to decipher the dominant themes, and identification, of the trade-offs and tensions that participants expressed in the data. In addition, in analyzing the language, the use of metaphors is employed as a data-reducing technique.

In a mixed design, Creswell & Piano (2011) suggest that "mixing during the data analysis occurs when the qualitative strands are mixed during the stage of the research process when the researcher is analyzing the two sets of results together through a combined analysis" (p. 67). The mixing during the data analysis was employed around the major categories to provide the researcher with another tool to analyze and interpret the commonalities, similarities, and dissimilarities across all the data sets in order to gain further perspective on the results of the study.

Validity and Reliability

In analyzing the written data compiled during and after the interviews and observations, the researcher looked for common threads; specific similarities or differences were recorded. To ensure reliability, the same questions were asked under the same conditions in each interview. Similar criteria were applied when conducting each observation. It is believed that the researcher's knowledge and experience in this field were sufficient to justify the accuracy of the information gained. In addition, the quantitative data from the survey was compared with the qualitative data in order to ascertain validity. Although some facets of internal validity, such as instrumentation, could have possibly affected the data, particularly, in the field observations, it is believed that is was reasonably controlled through triangulation of the following: field observations, focus group, survey, and interviews. In all situations, the data were consistent with respect to the research question. Since the responses of the participants were consistent within each of the data instruments (survey, interviews, focus group, and field observations) the study has internal validity. This study also addressed external validity because of the diversity of school levels of the principals participating. There were elementary, middle, 6-12 secondary, high school, and transfer high school principals. Irrespective of the school level, the responses from the participants were similar and therefore perhaps generalized to the overall population of New York City principals.

Chapter Summary

This chapter outlined the mixed method of research, data collection procedures, and the analysis format that were used to explore the central research question: How do New York City school principals understand their role as school leaders within their school reform initiative? In addition, the goal and purpose of this study were outlined, and the protocols for interviews, focus group, field observations, and online surveys were presented in order to gain insight on the research question.

References

Cresswell, J. (2009) Research Design (3rd edition) Thousand Oaks, CA; Sage Publications

Cresswell, J. and Piano, Clark, V.L. (2011) Designing and Conducting Mixed Methods Research (2nd Edition) Thousand Oaks, CA; Sage Publications.

Krueger, R.A., and Casey, M.A. (2009) Focus Groups: A Practical Guide for Applied Research. London: Sage Publications.

Marshall, C. and Rossman, G.B. Designing Qualitative Research (4th edition) Thousand Oaks, CA: Sage Publications.

Maxwell, J. (2009) Qualitative Research and Design (2nd Edition). Thousand Oaks, CA : Sage Publications.

Miles, M.B. and Huberman, A.M. (1994) Qualitative Data Analysis, Thousand Oaks, CA: Sage Publications.

Saldana, J. (2009). The Coding Manual for Qualitative Research: London: Sage Publications

Spata, A.V. (2003) Research Methods: Science and Diversity. New York, NY John Wiley and Sons.

Tashkkari, A. and Teddlie, C. (2003) The Handbook of Mixed Methods in Social and Behavioral Research. Thousand Oaks, CA: Sage Publications.